PORTFOLIO / PENGUIN

THE TURN THE SHIP AROUND! WORKBOOK

A top graduate of the U.S. Naval Academy, L. David Marquet commanded the nuclear-powered, fast-attack submarine USS *Santa Fe* from 1999 to 2001. After implementing Intent-Based Leadership, not only did the *Santa Fe* go from worst to first in Navy retention and ratings, but also a highly disproportionate number of its officers and crew were promoted to leadership positions. Since leaving the Navy, David has worked with businesses worldwide to create environments where people feel valued and contribute their all. David is a lifetime member of the Council on Foreign Relations, has taught graduate-level leadership courses at Columbia University, and lives in Florida with his wife, Jane.

Andy Worshek served with David Marquet and was instrumental in the turn-around of the USS *Santa Fe*, told in the business bestseller *Turn the Ship Around!*, where he is prominently mentioned. Andy helped implement the Intent-Based Leadership™ methodology while serving as the sonar chief and eventually chief of the boat for the USS *Santa Fe*, and continued to develop the methodology in the Navy and as head of HR at a leading accounting firm. Andy now travels extensively, delivering keynotes and workshops on Intent-Based Leadership. In his free time, he enjoys being with his family and volunteering at rodeo events. Andy resides in Oklahoma with his wife, Leigh.

The Turn the Ship Around! Workbook

IMPLEMENT INTENT-BASED LEADERSHIP
IN YOUR ORGANIZATION

L. DAVID MARQUET

with Andy Worshek

PORTFOLIO / PENGUIN

PORTFOLIO / PENGUIN
An imprint of Penguin Random House LLC
375 Hudson Street
New York, New York 10014
penguin.com

The Turn the Ship Around! Workbook first published by Portfolio / Penguin,
a member of Penguin Group (USA) LLC 2015
This revised and expanded edition published by Portfolio / Penguin,
an imprint of Penguin Random House LLC 2018.

Most Portfolio books are available at a discount when purchased in quantity for sales promotions or
corporate use. Special editions, which include personalized covers, excerpts, and corporate imprints, can be
created when purchased in large quantities. For more information, please call (212) 572-2232 or e-mail
specialmarkets@penguinrandomhouse.com. Your local bookstore can also assist with discounted bulk
purchases using the Penguin Random House corporate Business-to-Business program. For assistance in
locating a participating retailer, e-mail B2B@penguinrandomhouse.com.

ISBN 9780525534693 (trade paperback)

Printed in the United States of America
5   6   7   8   9   10

Set in Adobe Garamond
Designed by Spring Hoteling

CONTENTS

Imagine a World . . . | 1

PART I
. . . .
MECHANISMS FOR STARTING OVER

Chapter 1 | 13
Think Anew About Leadership

Chapter 2 | 19
Think Long-term, Even Beyond Your Tenure at the Organization

Chapter 3 | 25
Care but Don't Care

Chapter 4 | 31
Be Curious

Contents

Chapter 5 | 41
Do Something Different

Chapter 6 | 45
Create Leaders, Not Followers

Chapter 7 | 51
Achieve Excellence, Don't Just Avoid Errors

PART II

MECHANISMS FOR CONTROL

Chapter 8 | 71
Push Authority to Information

Chapter 9 | 79
Act Your Way to New Thinking

Chapter 10 | 89
Short, Early Conversations Make Efficient Work

Chapter 11 | 97
Use "I Intend to . . ." to Create Leaders at Every Level

Chapter 12 | 111
Return the Problem Unsolved

Chapter 13 | 117
Eliminate Top-Down Monitoring Systems

Chapter 14 | 123
Think Out Loud

Contents

Chapter 15 | 129
Embrace the Inspectors

PART III
....

MECHANISMS FOR COMPETENCE

Chapter 16 | 137
Take Deliberate Action

Chapter 17 | 143
We Learn (Everywhere, All the Time)

Chapter 18 | 149
Don't Brief, Certify

Chapter 19 | 157
Continually and Consistently Repeat the Message

Chapter 20 | 163
Specify Goals, Not Methods

PART IV
....

MECHANISMS FOR CLARITY

Chapter 21 | 171
Take Care of Your People and Build Trust

Chapter 22 | 177
Use Your Legacy for Clarity

Contents

Chapter 23 | 181
Use Guiding Principles for Decision Criteria

Chapter 24 | 185
Immediately Reward Desired Behaviors

Chapter 25 | 191
Begin with the End in Mind

Chapter 26 | 197
Encourage a Questioning Attitude over Blind Obedience

Chapter 27 | 203
Implementing Intent-Based Leadership and Building Leaders
at Every Level

PART V

. . . .

FINAL MECHANISM AND CONCLUSIONS

Chapter 28 | 209
Don't Empower, Emancipate

Chapter 29 | 215
Ripples

Intent-Based Leadership Manifesto | 217

Appendix: Summary of Practices from *Turn the Ship
Around!* | 219

Acknowledgments | 221

The
Turn the Ship Around!
Workbook

Imagine a World . . .

Imagine a workplace where everyone engages and contributes their full intellectual capacity, a place where people are healthier and happier because they have more control over their work—a place where everyone is a leader.

Unfortunately, many people do not find fulfillment in their work. For them, the workday is something to be tolerated. Their prime objective is a negative one—to avoid errors, problems, and confrontations. As a result, they do not put their full passion and intellect into their work, and a vast portion of the cognitive capacity of humankind is left idle.

Our mission is to change all that.

This is possible, but not with the current leadership paradigm. With the current paradigm, leaders do the thinking and order giving and followers do the doing and order following. When something goes amiss, we exhort leaders to give better orders and exhort followers to follow orders better. This approach marginalizes the very thing that makes us most human: our

1

ability to think, imagine a better future, and make decisions. The solution is not to give better orders but to create organizations where everyone thinks of themselves as leaders and makes decisions. In other words, in the highest performing organizations, leaders stop giving orders and create an environment where people don't need to be told what to do.

The book *Turn the Ship Around!* tells the story of the reinvention of leadership aboard the nuclear-powered submarine USS *Santa Fe.* I describe how small but fundamental changes in the way we talked to one another and treated one another resulted in a tenfold improvement in performance that endured well past my tenure as commanding officer. The idea was that by giving control to people, they become leaders.

It worked.

The *Santa Fe* achieved excellence in operations while I was its captain, winning numerous awards. More important, the people aboard the *Santa Fe* were selected at significantly disproportionate rates to higher leadership positions, including ten subsequent nuclear-submarine captains and six "major commanders"—the command position above submarine captain, such as a submarine squadron commodore.

The basic assumption is this: excellence is achieved when everyone is thinking. It is a framework that applies to all types of organizations—from submarines operating in the depths of the ocean to major corporations in city skyscrapers, and everywhere in between.

The leader's challenge is to decide how much control to give each person and to give the team.

I can assert this is true because people have told me. They've reported value creation of millions of dollars. They've improved performance measures such as productivity and safety. They've improved cultural measures such as employee turnover and engagement scores. They've grown their businesses. They've reported improved relationships with their family members and children and less stress in the household and at work. One lady, a

Figure 1a

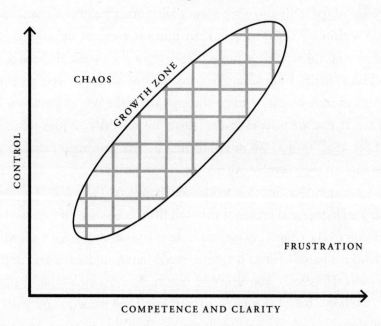

CHAOS

GROWTH ZONE

CONTROL

FRUSTRATION

COMPETENCE AND CLARITY

stress eater who had a significant job as the operations manager for more than a dozen restaurants, told me she lost fifty pounds because she was able to reduce the stress in her life.

While this workbook will discuss the mind-sets behind Intent-Based Leadership, its focus is on the mechanisms we will use to build Intent-Based Leadership organizations. In many cases this will boil down to language, the words we say. One of the grounding mind-sets is that the control a leader can give their team is dependent upon the team's competence and clarity. The main mechanism we use for this is the Ladder of Leadership.

While inviting people up the Ladder of Leadership, we remain vigilant to ensure that the underlying conditions for success are present: competence and clarity. This is how we give up control without creating chaos. Chaos is bad, especially on a nuclear submarine.

The Turn the Ship Around! Workbook

This workbook is designed to be a companion to *Turn the Ship Around!* It is designed for individuals who work with other people. No matter their position within the organization, their purpose remains the same: help the people around them achieve more. While it may be worked through as an individual activity, I encourage you to involve others as you go through this. A good start would be to go through the questions and activities with a partner. If you are a team leader, there are several activities that are designed for small teams. We've found that people gain more, change more, and do more if they involve others.

The organization of this workbook parallels *Turn the Ship Around!* chapter for chapter and proceeds through the mechanisms introduced there. In addition to the chapter questions, activities and tools have been added.

Change is hard. I felt as if I were forced into it under life-and-death circumstances. Hopefully, you won't be put in that situation—but it may feel like it. The best advice I can give is to start small and work on one small thing until it becomes your normal way of acting. Then, add another. And another.

In addition to adding more activities and clarifying others, there are two additions to this second revision. We've added several notes describing scientific research that supports the mechanisms of Intent-Based Leadership. These were added by organizational psychologist Dr. Michael Gillespie. You will find these sections labeled "RESEARCH PERSPECTIVE."

Additionally, Andy Worshek, one of the chiefs on board the USS *Santa Fe* whom I wrote about in *Turn the Ship Around!* has added his perspective. The chiefs on a submarine are the middle managers who have served as good technicians and been promoted to leadership positions. They are frontline leaders, interacting daily, even hourly, with their sailors and with the equipment used to run the submarine. You will find these sections labeled "CHIEF'S PERSPECTIVE." In these sections Andy shares some challenges of working with this approach from the middle of the organization.

Imagine a World . . .

CHIEF'S PERSPECTIVE

Our world radically changed when our mind-set shifted from avoiding errors to achieving excellence. Though it seemed to some like just a change in language, it resulted in a change in behavior. When we focused on how well we could learn from mistakes, and not on who to blame for mistakes, individual effort exploded. When we were given control over our work, the culture in the workplace dramatically changed.

Not everyone responded the same. Working the Intent-Based Leadership way requires that the boss give control and it requires that the team display their competence and clarity. In the situations we experienced where competence or clarity levels were not quite high enough for the group to be given control, the group's response was critical. The biggest barrier we experienced was a lack of clarity. Like a piece of information that maybe didn't get shared at all levels, or in some cases a lack of clarity as to what success looked like. Improving that clarity took courage on the boss's part. It is easy to just fix a problem, rather than help develop someone, but Intent-Based Leadership requires a long-term view. Having the courage to take the time to provide clarity meant that in the future teams were much more efficient and effective because they already had clarity of purpose.

WHY?

In the foreword to *Turn the Ship Around!* Stephen Covey wrote:

> We are in the middle of one of the most profound shifts in human history, where the primary work of mankind is moving from the Industrial Age of "control" to the Knowledge Worker Age of "release." As Albert Einstein said, "The significant problems we face cannot be solved at the same level of thinking we were at when we created them." They certainly won't be solved by one person; even, and especially, the one "at the top."
>
> Our world's bright future will be built by people who have discovered that leadership is the enabling art. It is the art of releasing human talent and potential. You may be able to "buy" a person's back with a paycheck, position power, or fear, but a human being's genius, passion, loyalty and tenacious creativity are *volunteered* only. The world's greatest problems will be solved by passionate, unleashed "volunteers."

Up till recently, leadership has been about getting people to do things. Getting people to do things can be done through command, compulsion, and compliance. Those who were the best at getting others to do things were promoted or created great establishments. They got rich and we wrote books about them.

What we need now is thinking. Since thinking, along with genius, passion, loyalty, and tenacious creativity, can't be compelled, our long-perfected leadership practices geared toward getting people to do must be upended.

Imagine a World . . .

In the next section, we start with a question: What are the greatest things that human beings achieve, and what are the characteristics of those acts?

ACTIVITY: ACT OF GREATNESS

The purpose of this activity is to think about the conditions under which humans do great things—by great things I mean those things that make your heart feel good.

Think of an act of greatness you may have witnessed or read about and write it down.

Pay For my collge = Sidney Hinton

If you are with a group, share your stories.

Consider the characteristics of that act. Did the people act for themselves or for another? Was the act ordered or self-initiated?

Another : Self-initiated

_____

_____

_____

If you are like most people, the act you recalled was about someone doing something for another person and was self-directed. In other words, acts of greatness are not ordered. Since they cannot be ordered, we consider them serendipitous. If they happen, we celebrate.

I believe that every human has the potential to do great things. We all have a latent superhero within. All too often, however, that superhero never sees the light of day because of fear, bureaucracy, or insecurities we carry with us.

Here's the Intent-Based Leadership challenge: What if, by the way we treated each other and by the way we talked to each other, we created environments that not only invited that superhero to action—not ordered it to action—but simply made it easier for people to embrace their inner superheroes? In many cases this means removing the fear most of us live with: fear of embarrassment, fear of failure, fear of getting fired. For all of us, it means creating environments free from fear that instead are safe for that inner superhero to be summoned forth.

Leadership is 20 percent knowledge and 80 percent behavior. Take charge of your leadership behavior by changing actions this week. Complete the following nudge this week:

....

 Personally deliver a message to someone to whom you are grateful for something he or she has done.

Imagine a World . . .

Who: _Demokian_   _Jennifer_

What: _Provided options (_   _) Agile Program_ / _Let's do it_

When: _Email last week._   _Last week_

....

Enroll in our leadership nudges—short sixty-second leadership nuggets delivered to your in-box—at www.davidmarquet.com. We now have over 150 of these archived on our YouTube channel: Leadership Nudges. These short videos are reminders of the things you've read in the workbook and are easy to share with your team. On the channel, you will see various play-lists, including a playlist called "Leadership Nudges: The Turn the Ship Around! Workbook." This playlist includes all the nudges covered in this workbook.

PART I
Mechanisms for Starting Over

High Look:
    A "high look" on a submarine means coming a foot or two shallower when the ship is at periscope depth. This puts the optics of the periscope a foot or two higher above the surface of the ocean, which allows us to see farther. In the workbook, a high look means we will step back to assess our progress.

....

CHIEF'S PERSPECTIVE

Our chiefs were at the level of our organization that was responsible for executing our organization's intent. We had a unique perspective as the ones who had extensive experience and influence up and down the organization. Stepping back for a "high look" was often helpful to explain, big picture, what we were trying to achieve.

....

....

Building on the desire to create an environment where people think rather than do, and recognizing that the greatest things we achieve as humans are not ordered, we need to change our leadership practices.

In this section we reimagine the role of leaders from bosses who take control and attract followers to leaders who give control and create more leaders.

....

Chapter 1
Think Anew About Leadership

What is your image of a leader? My images of leaders were formed by reading classics like *Beowulf* and *The Odyssey*, studying histories of the sea, and watching popular movies. The idea of the leader as an individual hero was strongly reinforced when I got to the U.S. Naval Academy.

We call this "know all—tell all" leadership. While captain of the USS *Santa Fe*, I transitioned through all four quadrants of the knowing/telling matrix but ended up believing that being a "know all—tell not" leader was the most helpful, empowering, and powerful place to operate.

Unfortunately, the "know all—tell all" leader minimizes the value and contributions of everyone else in the organization. I didn't realize it at the time, but the assumption behind this leadership structure, so fundamental that it has become subconscious, is that there are leaders and there are followers. It was only after I cleared my mind of these preconceptions that I was able to see a truly better way for humans to interact.

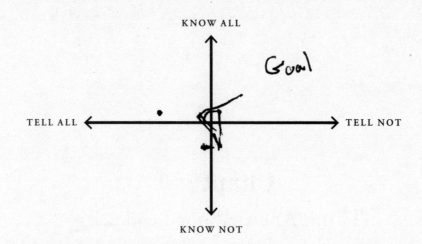

KNOW ALL

Goal

TELL ALL ← → TELL NOT

KNOW NOT

The pain of my time aboard USS *Will Rogers* was born of the leader-follower model (pages 8–10).

MECHANISM: IDENTIFY YOUR ASSUMPTIONS AND QUESTION YOUR PRECONCEPTIONS OF LEADERSHIP

QUESTIONS
Why do we need empowerment?

To give individual the space to become headers.

_____

_____

How does it feel when someone tries to "empower" you?

Disempowering - No one can empower
you. They may motivate you but that
is not sustainable.

_____

_____

_____

How reliant is your organization on the decision making of one person or of a small group of people? What is the impact of that?

Very
Impact! - lack of confidence + very little
thinking

_____

_____

_____

What kind of leadership model does your business or organization use?

Is say Relational, but in reality it:
Top Down or "leader - Follower.

_____

_____

_____

_____

_____

When you think of movie images that depict leadership, who and what come to mind? What are the behaviors of these leaders?

Hero - Sylh heahn
Command + Control

_____

_____

_____

_____

What assumptions are embedded in these images?

One person has all the answers
+ must be there to save the
day

_____

_____

_____

How do these images influence how you think about yourself as a leader?

That I have to be the one
who does all the thinking + doing.

_____
_____
_____
_____

To what extent do these images limit your growth as a leader?

I am not able to get out of the day
trap + it probably.
hinders my time to devop other leads.

The frustrations and pain you have felt either as a subordinate or as a leader will be what propels you toward creating a better world for yourself and the people around you. If you've ever felt you have more to contribute, if you've ever had the thought that you were the only person thinking at your company, then you've been subjected to the inadequacies of the traditional leader-follower approach to treating other people.

....

CHIEF'S PERSPECTIVE

My perspective of leadership revolved around two different ideals. The first was that of an achiever. My experience had been that a leader is someone who makes great decisions. We refer to that person as a "know all—tell all" leader. The second perspective was that a leader is someone who creates an environment where others can and do make great decisions. Knowing and recognizing when I acted in one of those roles was important to create an environment that invites people to act as leaders. When I was expending my energy on telling people what to do, I was simply creating followers. When I focused on my environment and started helping my teams with growing their <u>competence and clarity</u>, I saw dramatic changes in the way they approached our tasks.

....

....

👉 At the end of the day, mentally review your conversations and meetings, and look back through your sent e-mails. Write down the times where you told someone what to do. Include the times you used phrases like "Don't you think we should . . ."

_____

_3_____

_____

_____

_____

....

Chapter 2

Think Long-term, Even Beyond
Your Tenure at the Organization

A re you and your people working to optimize the organization for your tenure or forever? To promote long-term success, you need to ignore the short-term reward systems.

 The captain of the USS *Olympia* had no incentive to make sure the ship ran well after he departed (pages 11–14).

MECHANISM: THINK LONG-TERM

QUESTIONS

In your organization, in what ways are people rewarded for what happens after they depart? If they are not rewarded, how could they be?

_____

_____

_____

_____

_____

_____

Are they rewarded for the success of their people? What effect do you think rewarding behavior in this way would have on an organization?

_____

_____

_____

_____

_____

_____

Do people want to be missed after they leave? Why do you think this happens, and what effect do you think it has on the work environment?

_____

_____

_____

_____

_____

_____

When an organization does worse immediately after the departure of a leader, what does this say about that person's leadership? How does the organization view this situation?

_____

_____

_____

_____

_____

_____

How does the perspective of time horizon affect our leadership actions?

_____

_____

_____

_____

_____

What can we do to incentivize long-term thinking?

_____

_____

_____

_____

_____

_____

Since all investments in people are long-term investments, only those with a long-term perspective will see its value. We need to match the mindset with actions that reward decisions made for the long term and not the short term. This usually means making decisions that actually reduce short-term performance in favor of building capacity for the long term.

The idea is not to give a speech about long-term thinking but to come up with mechanisms that coax people toward long-term thinking. One possibility is to evaluate departing leaders a year following their departure based on how well the organization they left is doing. Another way is to make explicit what time frame decisions are optimized for.

When we operate in "know all—tell all" mode we are operating for short-term performance. When we operate in "know all—tell not" mode, we are thinking for the long term because we are forgoing short-term progress in order to build leaders for the future.

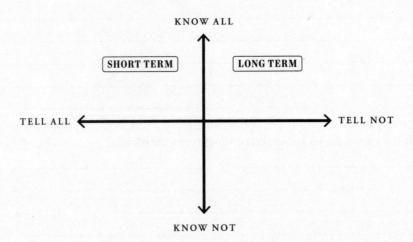

Think Long Term

....

CHIEF'S PERSPECTIVE

One mechanism the chiefs used to develop the skill sets of their teams was to look at the expected makeup of the team six months, one year, and two years from today. Since all sailors are assigned projected departure dates upon arrival, we could plan for the departure of people with key skills and schools. Having that perspective helped determine our direction. Oftentimes this traded short-term performance for long-term improvements to the team's capabilities. Oftentimes we struggled with the thought that if we invested in our teams long term, they would just take that talent elsewhere. To succeed in this perspective change we had to focus our risk analysis to this: what if we didn't invest in their training and they stayed?

....

....

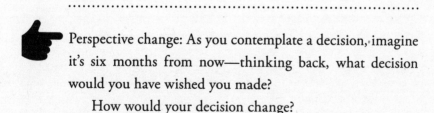 Perspective change: As you contemplate a decision, imagine it's six months from now—thinking back, what decision would you have wished you made?

How would your decision change?

_____

_____

_____

Perspective change: Write down where your expected team will be one year from today.

_____

_____

_____

_____

. . . .

Chapter 3
Care but Don't Care

When I was reassigned from the USS *Olympia* to the USS *Santa Fe*, I knew I needed a totally different leadership approach. Many leaders talk about getting the right people on board. The Navy has a system for recruiting people, but I didn't have any control over which of those people were assigned to the *Santa Fe*. I had the people I had. Not only that, but I had no control over which positions they went into. Each person arrives with an assignment to fill a specific job. This was a powerful constraint that both forced and allowed me to focus all my effort on changing how we talked to each other and how we treated each other. I focused my effort on creating an environment where the people I had could be their best.

It turns out this constraint luckily forced me to pay attention to the biggest determinant of team performance, now backed by research. Google conducted a study, Project Aristotle, to assess the key determinants of team performance. It turns out that the Google researchers found that how the team interacted had greater impact than who was on the team or what positions they were in.*

....

*https://rework.withgoogle.com/guides/understanding-team-effectiveness.

The other neat thing about this finding is that it involves everyone, as everyone has the ability to impact how we treat each other. Everyone can be involved, and culture is an "everyone" project.

Leaders should take stock of their level of commitment. I discovered that the hardest thing about my planned turnaround project was my own fortitude. In order to maintain my commitment, I had to adopt the idea of "care but don't care." Care deeply, passionately, intensely about the team and our mission; care not a lick about the bureaucratic consequences to myself. In other words, I didn't worry about whether I would get promoted, awarded, or criticized as a result of my actions.

....

CHIEF'S PERSPECTIVE

When you are working from somewhere in your organization other than the CEO's desk, you are still influencing up and down the hierarchy. Breaking the thought barriers that kept me tied to that internal competition we experience in our organizations unleashed a level of commitment that I had previously not experienced. We often hear this: just do what is right and your organization will take care of you. Whether or not you feel this is happening to you, great leaders apply this practice to their teams. When you are leading a department, a group, or a team, care intensely about their development and their growth. Let them know that they are valued. Take care of them. As a team member, let your commitment and excellence rise even when circumstances are not ideal.

....

I had to rethink my leadership approach after being assigned to the USS *Santa Fe* (pages 17–21).

MECHANISM: CARE BUT DON'T CARE

QUESTIONS

What are the practices by which you live your life? Are you ready to invest in people—long-term investments that may not pay off?

_____

_____

_____

_____

_____

_____

_____

What beliefs hold leaders back mentally and emotionally from giving up control?

_____

_____

_____

_____

_____

_____

_____

What do you anticipate will be the hardest thing you will experience when you let go of micromanaging, top-down leadership, or the cult of personality?

_____

_____

_____

_____

_____

_____

_____

How can you get your project teams interacting differently while still using the same resources?

_____

_____

_____

_____

_____

_____

What can you as a subordinate do to get your boss to let you try a new way of handling a project?

_____

_____

_____

_____

_____

_____

_____

When you delegate to your people, to what degree do you specify the steps you want accomplished and how much do you specify the goal you are trying to achieve? Explore an example here, including the goal and the terms for meeting that goal.

_____

_____

_____

_____

_____

_____

I can't tell you how many times I questioned whether I was on the right track and whether I should just go back to "command and control." At the time, no one knew if we were going to be successful. No one knew the impact of what we'd achieve in ten years. We just had faith that treating everyone better, like leaders, would work out in the long run. And it did.

....

CHIEF'S PERSPECTIVE

When you give control, your team will respond. Some team members will fully embrace the opportunity to display their competence and clarity, while others will be a bit hesitant. They will worry that they will make a mistake that will cost them their position. We did make mistakes, but the perseverance and commitment our top-level leaders displayed

29

helped us to learn and grow at an amazing pace. For many of us, the opportunity to control more of our work, to be valued, and to contribute was incredibly freeing. The psychological ownership shifted to our shoulders. It motivated many of us to freely give our excellence. I had previously witnessed individuals who would comply with the requirements of the job, but would hesitate to "go the extra mile." Some of your team will relish the opportunity to have that responsibility, and some will be hesitant but grow into the role. Take that first step and give control when you are the leader. Take on the challenge of displaying your competence and clarity when you are in the team member role. The results will surprise you.

....

My own preconceptions of leadership also got in the way. There were lots of movies about the kind of leader I didn't want to be, but I couldn't find any about the leader I wanted to be.

Here's an activity for movie buffs like me: Pick some movies to watch with your group and deconstruct the leadership paradigm. If you find Intent-Based Leadership in a movie, let me know.

....

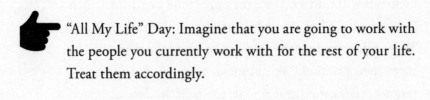

"All My Life" Day: Imagine that you are going to work with the people you currently work with for the rest of your life. Treat them accordingly.

....

Chapter 4
Be Curious

Are you curious? I thought I was being curious during my previous tours; turns out I was only "questioning." Leaders know they don't see everything. They are curious about what others see and think.

I had less than four weeks before I took command of the *Santa Fe*. While I was tempted to focus on learning the technical aspects of the ship, I decided to understand what was happening with the people instead. Why was the submarine performing so poorly, and why was morale so low?

Since all fifty of the Navy's attack submarines had the same schedule, same people with the same rank and pay structure, same schooling, same budgets, same purpose, and same support, why was it that this submarine was so much worse off than the others? I walked around asking questions like these:

- What are the things you hope I don't change?
- What are the things you secretly hope I do change?
- What are the good things about the *Santa Fe* we should build on?

- If you were me, what would you do first?
- Why isn't the ship doing better?
- What are your personal goals for your tour here on the *Santa Fe*?
- What impediments do you have to doing your job?
- What will be our biggest challenge to getting the *Santa Fe* ready for deployment?
- What are your biggest frustrations about how the *Santa Fe* is currently run?
- What is the best thing I can do for you?

 Not knowing the technical details of the USS *Santa Fe* caused me to appreciate curiosity (pages 22–27).

CHIEF'S PERSPECTIVE

We were used to having "know all—tell all" leaders: bosses that we perceived only asked a question to display their own intellectual superiority, test our knowledge, and put us on the defensive. It seemed as though we had to continually be ready to defend our knowledge or abilities, rather than grow our skill sets and mastery. I lost count of the number of times I felt like my bosses were asking questions just so they could find a reason to show me how smart they were. It was incredibly frustrating and meant people spent time trying to figure out what—oftentimes a trivial piece of information—our boss might have picked up. When our leader started asking questions from the "tell me more" perspective it released a level of learning in the organization that made us all smarter. Many times we think that if our leader says "I don't know" we have a bad leader. When our leader said "I don't know, let's figure it out," our energy shifted from defending what we knew to aggressively pursuing more knowledge and ability.

....

MECHANISM: BE CURIOUS

QUESTIONS

Do you have to be the smartest person in the room? Explain in what ways you find this to be true or false about yourself and how you think it affects your relationships with your people.

_____

_____

_____

_____

_____

_____

To what degree does technical competence form the basis for leadership?

_____

_____

_____

_____

_____

_____

Do you believe that technical competence is a personal competence or an organizational competence? Defend your answer.

_____
_____
_____
_____
_____
_____

How do you know what is going on in the front lines of your organization?

_____
_____
_____
_____
_____
_____

How do you let your boss know what is going on in the front lines of your organization?

_____
_____
_____
_____
_____
_____

Be Curious

I'm not endorsing not knowing how to do your job. In my case, it took a significant degree of ignorance to shift from questioning to being curious. It's better to know your job intimately while also being curious. That's what we call the "know all—tell not" quadrant of leadership. A more nuanced perspective would actually be to be a "learn all" leader rather than "know all," but the important thing is to resist, when possible, telling people what to do.

I had to train myself to recognize that the people telling me things that sounded new, different, unexpected, and wrong were the people giving me the most valuable information.

ACTIVITIES: *MASTER AND COMMANDER*

The purpose of these activities is to look anew at leadership and explore the negative impacts of what seems on the surface to be "good" leadership. As an expert leader you set the environment for people around you to achieve greatness. This is a good group activity.

What do I see?	Reality. How we interact with each other.
What do I do?	Be aware; see; listen.

You will need a copy of the movie *Master and Commander,* seven minutes of which we will watch in small increments throughout these activities.

ACTIVITY 1

1. The story of *Master and Commander* takes place on a British warship in 1805, and the main characters in the scenes we will be watching include Captain Jack Aubrey (Russell Crowe), First Lieutenant Thomas Pullings (James D'Arcy), and Midshipman Hollom (Lee Ingleby). In order to set up the context for the rest of the activities, watch the two-minute segment starting at 2:06 and ending at 4:00.

2. Now watch the scene from 4:00 to 4:13, which depicts a ship under way. Simply observe what is going on. At the end of the clip we will ask you to write down what you saw. This is Description and matches Level 2 "I see . . ." on the Ladder of Leadership.

3. After you have watched the clip, take one minute to write down what you see about this ship and its operating conditions.

_____

_____

_____

_____

_____

_____

Now compare your answers. What did others notice that you didn't?

As individuals we process scenes very quickly from observation to action:
Observation → Interpretation → Action
When we assemble in groups the natural tendency is to do the same.

Be Curious

We individually process from observation to interpretation to action. Then we all discuss what we should do (the action step) without understanding what we've all seen and interpreted.

More useful, however, is to defer the action phase of the meeting until after we all know what we've all seen and interpreted. Yes, this takes longer, but it is much more likely to result in a better decision.

So rather than this:

☺ Observation → Interpretation → Action ⎫
☺ Observation → Interpretation → Action ⎬ Discuss what action we should take
☺ Observation → Interpretation → Action ⎪
☺ Observation → Interpretation → Action ⎭

Meetings look more like this:

☺ Observation	Interpretation	Action	Discuss what action we should take
☺ Observation	Interpretation	Action	
☺ Observation	Interpretation	Action	
☺ Observation	Interpretation	Action	
	Discuss what we all see	Discuss what we all interpret	

4. Based on this activity, what is one thing you can do tomorrow when interacting with your people?

_____

_____

_____

_____

_____

_____

Lessons from Activity 1

- Not everyone sees the same things.
- No one sees what everyone sees.
- If you see something, say something. Don't assume that others see the same thing.
- The job of the leader is not to get people to agree upon an action but to make sure we all see what we all see, think what we all think, and know what we all know.

ACTIVITY 2

1. Watch from 4:13 to 5:08, as Mr. Hollom receives a report and reacts to it.

2. Give yourself one minute to write down your observations of Mr. Hollom's physical and emotional reaction to the report based on his facial expressions and body language.

_____

_____

_____

_____

_____

_____

Compare with others in your group.

Would you describe Mr. Hollom as curious? Is there anyone in the scene who appears curious?

Lessons from Activity 2

- We see only what we have words for. This is especially true for emotions.
- Fear reduces curiosity.

....

 "Know Nothing" Day: Tomorrow, assume some technological change has made everything you know about your job irrelevant. Now you know nothing. See how that impacts the way you talk to people.

Hint: You might want to tell the people you are working with that you are trying some new things.

....

Chapter 5

Do Something Different

When was the last time you walked around your organization to hear about the good, the bad, and the ugly of top-down management?

I saw the frustration in the officers and crew on the USS *Santa Fe* as a result of leader-follower (pages 28–34).

MECHANISM: ASK IF YOU CAN START IMPLEMENTING INTENT-BASED LEADERSHIP IN YOUR ORGANIZATION (EVEN IF YOU ARE THE BOSS!); YOU CAN'T ORDER PEOPLE TO PARTICIPATE IN AN EMPOWERMENT PROGRAM.

QUESTIONS

Where is the pain and frustration greatest in your organization? What frustrations do the "bosses" have with the workers? What frustrations do the workers have with the bosses?

_____

_____

_____

_____

_____

_____

In your workplace, do you believe people lean more toward desiring change or toward simply being comfortable with the current level of performance? Why do you think this is, and what do you think is the ideal state for a workplace?

_____

_____

_____

_____

_____

_____

Do Something Different

How would you describe the culture of your workplace? How prevalent are behaviors that support others in the organization and achieve progress?

_____

_____

_____

_____

_____

_____

In what ways does leadership in your organization take or give control?

_____

_____

_____

_____

_____

_____

You can't implement a bottom-up leadership approach in a top-down manner. Coercing people into an Intent-Based Leadership process would clearly violate the most fundamental principles of Intent-Based Leadership.

....

CHIEF'S PERSPECTIVE

The impact of your presence in your organization can be incredible. Walking through your office, shop floor, or organization can be very revealing. For us, having the leader talk with us in the places we worked was empowering. Not only did it spark conversation about how we could do things better, it made us feel like our work and efforts were valued. I saw two keys to these engagements. First, the visit was never an interrogation. It was always a conversation that was motivated by curiosity—the leader asking about how we were doing, asking about what we thought. In those interactions we also learned what the leader thought. Second, many of the interactions were solely motivated by the leader's desire to express gratitude for something we had worked at hard.

....

....

 The next time you get an e-mail from an employee reporting a problem without a solution, go talk to him and see if you can get him to come up with a solution. Here's an example of what you could say:

Thank you for bringing this important issue to my attention. I sincerely believe that this challenge is important, and you have demonstrated sufficient technical competence and organizational clarity to solve it. I'm depending on you to take the next steps. Please keep me informed about what you intend to do and if you need any help.

The next time you find a problem, and you bring it to the attention of your boss, try providing a solution as well. "Here's what I see and I think this might solve this problem." Here's an example of what to say:

Hey boss, I found this issue and I think we need to fix this. Here's how I see it and here is what I would like to do to fix it. I'll keep you informed.

....

Chapter 6
Create Leaders, Not Followers

What goes on in your workplace that reinforces the notion that the people at the top are the leaders and everyone else is simply to follow? I was startled to find this mentality was pervasive on the *Santa Fe*.

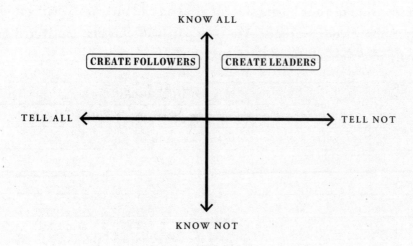

There was the petty officer on board the USS *Santa Fe* who told me his job was to do whatever they told him to do (page 36).

MECHANISM: CREATE LEADERS AT EVERY LEVEL

QUESTIONS

Why is doing what you are told so appealing to some? Do people really just want to do as they are told?

_____

_____

_____

_____

_____

_____

If a snapshot of your business went viral on the Internet, what would it reveal about your workers? Are they passive followers, motivated primarily to avoid making mistakes?

_____

_____

_____

_____

_____

_____

Create Leaders, Not Followers

Do your procedures reinforce the leader-follower model? In what ways are you either reinforcing or breaking away from this model?

_____

_____

_____

_____

_____

_____

How about implementing a "daily intentions" e-mail where team members state their intentions at the beginning of the day in an e-mail to the team leader and copy all team members. How about building on that to include a "what I achieved yesterday" section. What would such an e-mail from you to your supervisor look like?

_____

_____

_____

_____

_____

Other habits that reinforce the "do as you're told" approach include:

- Checking with bosses to get permission to go home.
- Weekly meetings where bosses review with subordinates what they "owe" them.

- Briefings where bosses told subordinates what was expected of them.
- Forms that required subordinates to get permission from bosses in order to act.
- Policy and governance documents that required bosses with specific rank or qualifications to make certain decisions.
- Review and update meetings where bosses asked questions to demonstrate their authority and knowledge rather than their curiosity and respect.
- Conversations where subordinates reported problems without solutions—the implication being that the boss should then direct a solution.
- Conversations where subordinates said, in effect, "Tell me what to do."

....

CHIEF'S PERSPECTIVE

Here is the incredible lesson: people will do exactly what they are told. If the environment in your workplace recognizes people at the top as leaders and everyone else as followers, that is generally how your teams will function. In caustic environments where mistakes are used to determine who keeps their job and who doesn't, people will do everything to avoid making a mistake. This means that usually they do only what they are told, because then they would not be making a mistake, they would just be doing what they were told. It leads to a bias toward inactivity. As leaders were created at every level on board the *Santa Fe* and mistakes were used as tools to learn and improve, people were willing to offer suggestions and observations, and started recommending courses of action. There's comfort in just doing what you are told—you don't carry any responsibility for the outcome!

....

....

 The next time an employee comes to you with "tell me what to do," ask them what they see or think. Some questions you might ask could be:

- If you were me, what would you be worried about?
- Can you describe the decision we need to make here?
- Can you describe the pros and cons of each decision?
- What do you hope or wish could happen here?
- If I weren't here, what would you do?

If you find yourself in a position where you feel like you might need the boss to tell you what needs to be done, try these questions:

- I don't want you to tell me what to do here, but can you provide more clarity?
- What would it look like if I succeeded at this?
- How can I be more successful?

Sometimes we learn that we need to build a new skill set or enhance an existing ability. It is important to be transparent in these cases and let the boss know what you are thinking.

....

Chapter 7
Achieve Excellence, Don't Just Avoid Errors

*It turns out that reducing errors is
a by-product of achieving excellence.*

There is a lot that you don't want to have happen on a nuclear submarine. You don't want to drop a torpedo. You don't want to melt down the reactor. You don't want to let water into the "people tank." Depending upon your profession, you probably want to avoid regulatory violations, safety violations and accidents, losing clients, or issuing defective products. The officers and crew on board the USS *Santa Fe* were highly biased toward avoiding mistakes, but the effect was an avoidance of decision making and a pervasive passivity throughout the organization. After all, the best way to avoid making mistakes is to do nothing, certainly not by making any decisions.

I find that many organizations define success in terms of a reduction of bad things: fewer recalls, fewer security violations, fewer injuries. The point is that none of these things inspires people to achieve greatness, and they bias the organization toward inactivity.

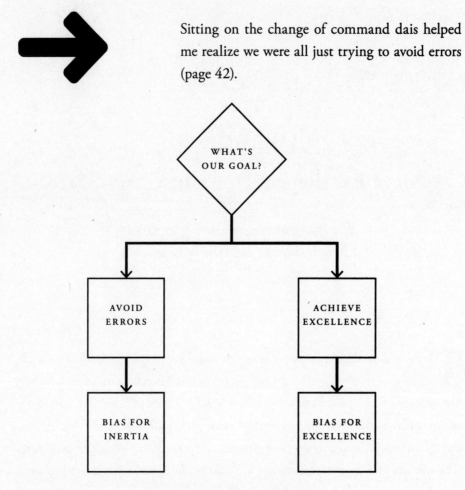

Sitting on the change of command dais helped me realize we were all just trying to avoid errors (page 42).

MECHANISM: ACHIEVE EXCELLENCE, DON'T JUST AVOID ERRORS

QUESTIONS
What do you see in terms of ways your people are trying to avoid making mistakes rather than trying to achieve excellence?

_____

_____

_____

_____

_____

_____

How have error-reduction programs reduced the incentive for initiative and risk taking? Explain the effects of this and how you could potentially revive initiative within your organization.

_____

_____

_____

_____

_____

_____

Have you ever spent more time critiquing errors than celebrating success? Write down the conversation exactly. What steps could you take to remedy this? Could this be applied to more conversations?

_____

_____

_____

_____

_____

_____

What do you see as some of the symptoms of avoiding errors in your workplace?

_____

_____

_____

_____

_____

_____

What do you see in terms of how people describe their jobs? To what degree do they frame it as achieving greatness or avoiding mistakes?

_____

_____

_____

_____

_____

_____

What has been the response of your organization to past errors? What has been the impact on the mind-set of the people in the organization?

_____

_____

_____

_____

_____

_____

Achieve Excellence, Don't Just Avoid Errors

When you investigate how decisions are made, what evidence do you see that the avoidance of negative outcomes outweighs accomplishing greatness? Provide some examples.

_____

_____

_____

_____

_____

_____

What is the primary motivation of the middle managers and frontline operators of your organization (not what it says on the poster outside the boardroom)?

_____

_____

_____

_____

_____

_____

How can you work to minimize errors in a way that does not make minimizing errors the focus of your organization?

_____

_____

_____

_____

_____

_____

_____

One way to think about the mind-set shift from avoiding errors to achieving excellence is to rethink your relationship with variability. In an environment where you want to control outcomes, such as in manufacturing, the objective is to reduce variability. We call this "red work."

However, when it comes to thinking, when it comes to innovation, when it comes to creativity, we want to embrace variability, not reduce it. We call this "blue work." Of course, in your organization there is not one clear answer. For many areas you want to reduce variability, and in others you want to embrace variability. The job of the leader is to know which is which. What we normally see is that organizations are fuzzy about what is red work and what is blue work. The result is often the application of the wrong protocols. Generally, since the industrial revolution was focused on red work, organizations are good at it. It's the blue work they need help with.

Repeating a stable and defined process is a reduce-variability activity. This happens in manufacturing, quick-service restaurants, health clinics, and a host of other organizations. These activities tend to be about "doing." Improving the process and discovering new activities are increase-variability activities, blue work. These activities tend to be about "thinking."

So here are a couple of ways to think about the red work/blue work model. The first is, who in your organization is doing red work and who is doing blue work? In traditional organizations, only a few people at the top are expected to do the thinking work and decision work, the blue work. Everyone else has been hired to execute the decisions of the leaders. Those people are expected to do the red work.

Achieve Excellence, Don't Just Avoid Errors

ACTIVITY 1

In teams, make a vertical line on a whiteboard or flip chart. On one side write down red work activities and on the other side write down blue work activities.

ACTIVITY 2

Where is the blue work/red work boundary and can we push it lower in the organization? Flip to a clean piece of paper.

The next way to think about it is to consider what kind of work you are doing over time. What we saw is that people move from one red work activity to another. We would move from surfacing the ship (a procedure) to entering port (another procedure) without any blue work. By injecting a decision—"are we ready to enter port?"—we would inject an element of blue work into the process. Then, once the decision was made, we'd be back to the red work. Moving from one medical procedure to another, or from one machine setup to another in manufacturing, are other examples. While some organizations have protocols for injecting an element of blue work they end up becoming pro forma.

ACTIVITY 3

When and how often are we doing blue work? Flip to a clean sheet. Can we increase the frequency of blue work? For example, is this a decision meeting (blue work) or simply a meeting to get everyone executing a predetermined plan (red work)?

....

CHIEF'S PERSPECTIVE

Knowing the difference between the reduce-variability and embrace-variability work is the key. When we worked in situations that had defined, tested, reliable, and written procedures, we focused on compliance with the procedures. (We address that in exercises in chapters 16 and 18.) When we needed to generate new processes or procedures we achieved excellence when we embraced variability. Communicating the desire to hear ideas, thoughts, and input to your team is critical. Listening without judging results in better input. There will be ideas and input that challenge the norm or have been tried before. Approach those ideas with a fresh perspective and look for circumstances that might have changed since the last time an idea was tried.

....

ACTIVITY 4: POLICY AS STORY

There's a tugboat company on the Great Lakes that moves barges up and down the lakes. The company does steady business in the spring, summer, and fall months but encounters issues in the winter when serious storms brew up and waves get high, making water travel perilous and important decisions necessary.

One of the key decisions the tugboat captains have to make is whether to get under way and move their 30,000-ton barges up and down the Great Lakes, depending on whether the weather is manageable or sufficiently bad to warrant staying in port. If the weather is getting bad and a captain makes the decision to move the barge, he puts himself and his crew in danger of potentially getting seriously injured or killed. If a captain decides not to get under way and the weather turns out not to be that bad, the company is in danger of losing business to the barge company across town.

Since the success of the company depends on safe transport and maintaining its client base, the decision of the tugboat captain is an important one. So what happens to address this? The first thing the company does is write a policy document that outlines what qualifies as weather bad enough to keep the ship in port.

For example, the company specifies that if the seas are going to be greater than eight feet, or if the wind will be more than 30 mph, the barges don't leave. But what if you have a situation where the seas are predicted to be more than eight feet but they are coming from astern and the tugboat captain believes that his crew can make the trip? Or there's another situation where the seas are only seven feet but the fetch, the distance between the waves, is very short, which makes for a more dangerous situation? So in some cases seven-foot seas can be too dangerous but nine-foot seas can be okay. While situational variation seems daunting at first and near impossible to write policy for, the company decided to have the tugboat captains write about the decisions they made, along with all the details leading up to the decision: here's what the weather was like; here's what I decided and why I decided it. Then the company collects these stories, and the CEO and CFO review and provide feedback. For example, after reviewing a story where the tugboat captain decided not to leave, the CEO and CFO have the information to let them know that their competitor sent barges out that day and as a result their tugboat company lost the business.

The point is to augment your policies with stories because, while people will forget what paragraph 2.1.57 details, they will remember details and the important lessons to be learned from stories. You want to move away from the prescriptive method—i.e., telling people what to do, to read the rules, and to follow the instructions—and instead move toward a thinking method.

1. After reading this account, your job as a leader will be to decide what areas of your company policy you want to emphasize and/or what areas you think

would gain clarity and help your people if they were fleshed out with stories. If you function as a team member in your organization, which company policies could you emphasize with a story? What are the key decisions that really determine success and failure in your organization?

2. Have your team write down a related story, one with a positive outcome and one with a negative outcome. Encourage them to think about all the relevant factors, including what external factors created or influenced the situation, what they decided, and their reasons for making the decision they did.

3. Review and annotate the stories, drawing attention to the longer-term consequences of the employee's decision and providing insight unique to his or her situation that the employee might not know or have taken into account.

4. Once all the stories have been compiled and annotated, create a book. You can use this book moving forward as a training tool for new employees or a reference for current employees on how to respond to any given situation. You should continually add new stories, update information, and have your employees be familiar with the contents.

 The next time a team member comes to you with an inspirational story, document it in some easy way (e.g., photo, short e-mail, blog post) and share it with your team. Encourage others to share their stories as well.

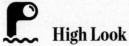 **High Look**

By now you should be thinking about what good leadership is. Key concepts so far include:

Achieve Excellence, Don't Just Avoid Errors

- Humans can achieve great things, but the greatest accomplishments are not ordered. You can't order your way to greatness.
- Humans are not inspired by the avoidance of errors; they are inspired by striving for excellence that connects them to other people. Don't avoid errors; achieve excellence.
- Leaders invest in people, and since all people investments are long-term investments, leaders think long-term. Leaders don't want to be missed after they leave.
- Leaders distinguish between reduce-variability activities and increase-variability activities.

There has been a fundamental change in the last century: a change from getting people *to do* to getting people *to think*. This, in turn, profoundly changes the way we should lead.

....

ACTIVITIES: *MASTER AND COMMANDER*

Now we will continue the *Master and Commander* activity.

ACTIVITY 5

1. Watch the scene from 5:08 to 6:20, which depicts Mr. Hollom grappling with a decision. Understanding the decision-making structure of your organization is the key to understanding the degree to which your organization makes leaders.

2. Why is the decision to beat to quarters so hard?

_____

_____

_____

_____

_____

_____

3. Which of Mr. Hollom's behaviors lead us to believe he is trying to achieve excellence or avoid errors?

_____

_____

_____

_____

_____

_____

Lessons from Activity 5

- The leader owns the environment. There are no people who "want to be told what to do," only people in environments that want to be told what to do. The environment matters a *lot*.

ACTIVITY 6

1. Watch from 6:20 to 7:55, pausing the video when Captain Jack Aubrey says, "Well, you did the right thing."

2. What does Mr. Hollom know that Captain Aubrey does not know?

_____

_____

_____

_____

_____

_____

3. What is the impact of the captain's interaction with Mr. Hollom?

_____

_____

_____

_____

_____

4. What is the likely impact on the rest of the officers?

_____

_____

_____

_____

5. Why does Mr. Hollom tell the captain he is sure when we know he is anything but?

_____

_____

_____

_____

_____

_____

Lessons from Activity 6

- The job of the leader is to uncover everything that everyone knows. The question "Are you sure?" does not accomplish this.
- Trust is not the same as competence. Trust means we are in it together and I believe that what you tell me is what you believe the actual state of nature to be. This does not mean that it _is_ the actual state of nature. That is a function of competence.

ACTIVITY 7

1. Continue watching until Captain Jack Aubrey comes up through the hatch and gets knocked down (about minute twelve). Watch Captain Aubrey as he marches forward. How many orders does he give? What about the order to the captain of marines to place sharpshooters "in the tops"? Why does the captain have to give this order? Write down your thoughts.

_____

_____

_____

_____

_____

_____

2. We end with the captain knocked down. What if Captain Aubrey doesn't get up? How do you think his crew will fare?

_____

_____

_____

_____

_____

_____

3. How would the answer to question 2 be different if Intent-Based Leadership had been implemented?

_____

_____

_____

_____

_____

_____

4. Based on this activity, what can you do differently tomorrow to make sure that if you get "knocked down" your people will continue to do well?

_____

_____

_____

_____

_____

_____

Lesson from Activity 7

- While we may be attracted to the bold and charismatic leader who confidently spouts off orders, we realize that this behavior fosters dependent followers. If what we want is to spawn additional leaders, then we need to let our people think for themselves, make decisions, and accept responsibility.

....

RESEARCH PERSPECTIVE

Focusing on error prevention is limiting. First of all, it's often impossible. Second, this emphasis reduces exploration and hinders learning. Instead, organizations can more fruitfully embrace errors as learning opportunities. This way, they can identify upstream contributions to the error and downstream ways of minimizing or eliminating the impact of the error. Van Dyck et al. (2005) investigated the effects of such an "error management culture" in two studies: one with sixty-five Dutch organizations and one with forty-seven German organizations. They found that managing errors and learning from them—as opposed to focusing primarily on error prevention—improves goal achievement, revenue, and profits.

Cathy van Dyck, Michael Frese, Markus Baer, and Sabine Sonnentag, "Organizational Error Management Culture and Its Impact on Performance: A Two-Study Replication," *Journal of Applied Psychology* 90, no. 6 (2005): 1228–40.

....

PART II
Mechanisms for Control

Control is about making decisions concerning not only how we are going to work but also toward what end. My primary focus when I assumed command of the *Santa Fe* was to divest control and distribute it to the officers and crew. The primary challenge for leaders on a short-term and long-term basis is to decide how much control to distribute to their teams. Our fundamental belief is that the amount of control ceded to the team and individuals must be tuned to the level of technical competence and organizational clarity that each member of the team has. It turns out that giving people control has significant benefits, from releasing their passion and engagement to improving health, weight, longevity, and quality of life.

In the Intent-Based Leadership way, leaders give as much control as they can based upon the competence and clarity of the team members, and then a little bit more. This is a critical point and the opposite of the way almost every organization we've encountered operates. Most organizations force their people to prove their competence and clarity before the leader gives additional control. The Intent-Based Leadership way is to do the opposite. Leaders, in small ways, sometimes imaginary ways, give control to their teams. They do this on a case-by-case basis by asking questions like "what do you think about this?" or "what would you do if you had to make this decision without me?" They also do this in a formal organizational way by changing decision rights. On the submarine we did both.

A submarine has a built-in structure whereby information is channeled up the chain of command to decision makers. We call this pushing information to authority. Instead, we deconstruct decision authority and push it down to where the information lived. We call this pushing authority to information. There are multiple benefits to this and it does not require any influence from the outside rules. It does, however, require the leader to trust first, and the team to act on the trust they've been given. Let us now turn back to figure 1a on page 3.

Figure 1a

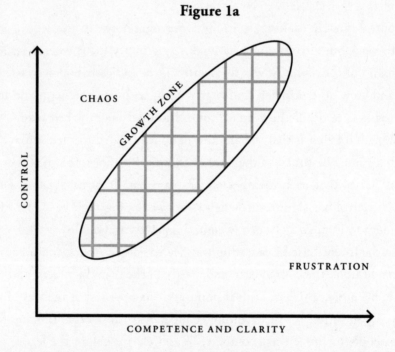

The chapters in this part will introduce you to the initial set of mechanisms we devised to divest control and implement Intent-Based Leadership practices.

The fundamental mind-set changes are:

- Give control, don't take control.
- Invite people up the Ladder of Leadership.

Mechanisms for Control

The mechanisms for control are as follows:

- Push authority to information, not information to authority.
- Act your way to new thinking.
- Short, early conversations make efficient work.
- Use "I intend to . . ." to turn passive followers into active leaders.
- Resist the urge to provide solutions.
- Eliminate top-down monitoring systems.
- Think out loud (both superiors and subordinates).

Chapter 8
Push Authority to Information

When we give people more authority, we create more leaders.

What's the best way to change decision-making authorities in your organization? Turns out it's pretty easy once you commit to changing. These decision-making authorities are embedded in your company's HR policy documents. Good news is that you have the ability to change them.

An example of this on the USS *Santa Fe* was the vacation policy. While Navy regulations specified that the executive officer sign the vacation requests for the enlisted men, we changed it so that the chief of the boat, the senior enlisted man, did it. This was a dramatic departure from practice and regulation as the chiefs typically followed the orders of the officers. By pushing the authority into the ranks of the chiefs, we not only assigned the decision making to the men who had the most immediate, relevant information, but we also dramatically empowered a group that was long on experience but short on authority.

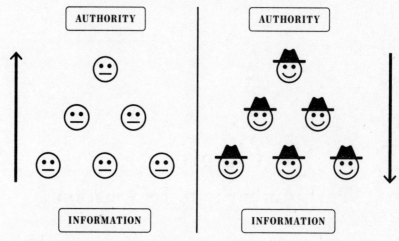

OLD WAY: Push Information to Authority   NEW WAY: Push Authority to Information

I changed the authority for vacation requests by authorizing the chiefs to sign the vacation requests for their sailors instead of pushing them to the executive officer (pages 56–58).

QUESTIONS

How can you prepare your mid-level managers to shift from holding a "position of privilege" to one of "accountability, responsibility, and work"? As a mid-level manager, how can you exercise accountability and responsibility for your work?

_____
_____
_____
_____
_____
_____
_____

What procedure or process can you change with a few words that will give your mid-level managers more decision-making authority?

_____
_____
_____
_____
_____
_____

When thinking about delegating control, what do you worry about?

_____
_____
_____
_____
_____
_____

What do you as a proponent of the Intent-Based Leadership approach need to delegate to show you are willing to walk the walk?

_____

_____

_____

_____

_____

_____

ACTIVITY: PUSH AUTHORITY TO INFORMATION

1.   Identify where decision-making authority is specified in the organization's policy documents.

2.   Identify decisions that are candidates for being pushed to the next lower level in the organization.

3.   For the easiest decisions, first draft language that changes the person who will have decision-making authority. In some cases, large decisions may need to be disaggregated.

4.   As a group, complete the following sentence on an index card: "When I think about delegating this decision, I worry that . . ."

5.   Post those cards on the wall, go on a long break, and let the group mill around the comments posted on the wall.

6.   Last, when the group reconvenes, sort and rank the worries and begin to attack them.

Push Authority to Information

When this activity is conducted, you will usually find that the worries fall into two broad categories: issues of competence and issues of clarity. People are worried that the next level down won't make good decisions, either because they lack the technical competence about the subject or because they don't understand what the organization is trying to accomplish. Both of these can be resolved.

The first step in pushing authority to information is documenting and then changing the way the organization controls decisions in an enduring, systemic way.

You can't "direct" empowerment programs. Directed empowerment programs are flawed because they are predicated on this assumption: I have the authority and ability to empower you (and you don't). Fundamentally, that's disempowering. This internal contradiction dooms these initiatives.

Rather, you should search for the organizational practices and procedures that would need to be changed in order to have the greatest leverage in giving people control and creating engaged workplaces. The goal is to implement enduring mechanisms that will embed the goodness of the organization in your people and practices and won't rely on any one person to make it happen.

However, distributing control by itself isn't enough. As that happens, it puts requirements on the new decision makers to have a higher level of operational knowledge and clearer sense of organizational purpose than ever before. That's because decisions are made against a set of criteria that includes what's operationally appropriate and what aligns with the organization's interests.

CHIEF'S PERSPECTIVE

We experienced many situations where we had the information at our level in the organization to make a decision, but lacked the authority. Moving authority downward can feel very risky for both the boss and the team. Even when we possessed the competence and clarity to make a decision, higher levels in the organization feared that we would make a decision that might only benefit our level in the organization. What actually happened was profound. Because the authority now rested on our shoulders, we took on the psychological ownership for the decision. We started to ask ourselves, is this how the boss would handle this? At first, I think we were a bit too conservative, a bit too risk averse in our decision processes.

At my level in the organization, some of us had been so conditioned to the idea that the captain is the only one to give orders that having the authority to make a decision felt like too much risk. This is not uncommon in situations where you can, by indecision, force someone higher in the hierarchy to deliver the bad news; to be the one who denies a request or demands rework or overtime. Having the ability to discuss the decision with our superiors without being told what decision to make was key for us building the confidence to execute this initiative. It is imperative that the lines of communication improve when authority is transferred. Too often, the approach can be that if I don't have to ask for permission, I don't need to inform anyone. The opposite is actually true and radically improved our efficiency and effectiveness.

Push Authority to Information

....

 The next time you are supposed to lead a meeting, don't go. Delegate it to your team. Have them tell you what happened after the meeting.

....

Chapter 9
Act Your Way to New Thinking

W hen you're trying to change employees' behaviors, you have basically two approaches to choose from: try to change their thinking and hope this leads to new behaviors, or try to change their behaviors and hope this leads to new thinking. It does not matter whether people think differently at some point as long as they behave in the desired and changed manner. There will be some employees who will never understand what you are trying to do and resist the change to Intent-Based Leadership, but if they will behave as if they believe, that is good enough.

For example, on the *Santa Fe* we wanted people to be "proud" of the ship. We could have gone about it by trying to somehow convince people to feel proud, and then hope that feeling spilled over into changed behaviors. That is not what we did. Instead, we tried to understand what it would look like from a behavioral basis to be on a team that people were proud of. We came up with a list of observable behavior. Then we picked one and tried to get the crew to act that way. We implemented the three-name rule when welcoming inspectors on board. The three-name rule consisted of this: when you saw a visitor or inspector on board the *Santa Fe* you would greet them with three names—your name, their name, and the name of the submarine: Good morning, Captain Smith. I am Petty Officer Martinez. Welcome aboard the USS *Santa Fe*. We didn't explain why, just asked them to try the new behavior as an experiment to see what would happen. The impression was a ship with good morale, but the way we got there wasn't by giving speeches about "being proud of your ship." It was by giving the crew a tool they could use to actually practice being proud.

The interesting thing was that immediately people visiting the ship noticed and remarked on the difference, even though only a small percentage of the crew practiced this new behavior. As several months passed, and more and more of the crew practiced this behavior, it began to feel more natural. What was happening was that the words we were repeatedly saying were rewiring our brains so that we actually felt proud of the submarine. The circle was closed, but it was the words that came first for most of us.

Implementing the "three-name rule" changed the way the crew thought (page 66).

QUESTIONS

What reasons do you hear for resisting change?

_____

_____

_____

_____

_____

_____

_____

What are some of the costs associated with doing things differently in your industry?

_____

_____

_____

_____

_____

Do you believe that you act first and think later or that you think first and then change your actions? Explain.

_____

_____

_____

_____

_____

_____

ACTIVITY: ACT YOUR WAY TO NEW THINKING

1. Starting condition: you've had a discussion with your leadership group and identified some sort of cultural change the group mostly agrees to.

What you want to do now is embed it into the organization, independent of personality.

2. Hand out index cards. Have people complete the following sentence: "I'd know we achieved [this cultural change] if I saw employees . . ." (The specific wording in this question should move you from general, immeasurable ones such as "Have people be creative" to specific, measurable ones such as "Employees submit at least one idea a quarter. The ideas are posted and other employees can comment on them.")

3. Allow five minutes. Then tape the cards on the wall, go on break, and have everyone mill around and allow them time to read the cards.

4. Based on the discussions and quantity of answers, you may want to give everyone a second shot at filling out another set of cards.

5. Sort and prioritize the answers.

6. Then discuss how to code the behavior into the company's practices.

7. Start practicing the new behavior.

8. Finally, write the new practices into the appropriate company procedure.

Here's an example from a high-tech company:

The company felt that respect was a core value and they wanted their people to "respect" each other more. Since the workshop was with frontline and above leaders the question became, what would leaders say that showed more respect? The company created a specific scenario: let's say someone working for you comes to you and tells you they intend to "turn right" and you are 99 percent sure that we should really "turn left." Now "turn right" and "turn left" are proxies and could be things like change a feature in a software product, change a maintenance schedule, change an advertising campaign, or any other decision.

To make it specific, the question was "what words coming out of the mouth of the leader next would show the greatest respect?" The group worked on a variety of responses, offered them up, and scored them from zero to five.

"No, turn right." Scores were zero to one. Very low in respect.

"No, turn right. Here's why . . ." Scores were zero, ones, and some twos. A little better.

"Why do you want to turn left?" Scores were higher: twos, threes, fours. Why not fives? Because "why" can put people on the defensive.

"Take me through your thinking." Higher scores. It's open-ended, neutral.

"Tell me more." High scores and my favorite.

So at the end the group decided that hearing more of "tell me more" would mean they were practicing the value of respect and so they resolved to try that. Since this was an observable behavior, they could check each other on the behavior and it was immediately noticed by the rest of the company. Soon, it became the cultural norm.

MECHANISM: ACT YOUR WAY TO NEW THINKING

Another way to think about it is this: you are actively engaged in changing habits. For example, most people like to solve problems, especially when other people bring them problems to solve. Habits, as Charles Duhigg reports in *The Power of Habit,* follow a cue and result in a reward. In this case the cue is another person asking you a question, and the reward is the good feeling that comes when you've answered it.

Unfortunately, while this habit feels good in the short term, it is deleterious to developing your people into leaders. When you solve people's problems for them, you deprive them of the opportunity to solve their own problems, to learn, and to develop into leaders.

Since it is very difficult to stop a habit (effectively replacing a habit with nothing), the key is to replace a habit with a more useful habit.

In the case of leadership, this means that when someone brings you a problem to solve, do not solve his or her problem. Instead, solve a different problem. The new problem is "How long can I wait before I have to solve this problem for them?" or even "How much can I risk if this person gets this totally wrong?"

....

CHIEF'S PERSPECTIVE

When tackling this issue the most effective way to adopt the new action is to set the example. One of the "acts" we adopted was to make the rule that we would refer to anyone onboard the *Santa Fe* as "we," and never "they." The result over time was that we started to actually think of one another as a "we." The most powerful act for us was when we saw our leaders refer to each other as "we." On board a submarine the engineering department and the weapons department exchanged a banter that played into the "we" versus "they" attitude. It had not been unusual to hear the respective department heads refer to each other as "they." When my department head was discussing an issue with me and he referred to the engineering department as "we," I was stunned, but also challenged to act in the same way.

If you do the above activity and have the courage to act on the behavior that comes from the "I'd know we achieved [this cultural change] if I saw employees . . ." activity, you will have the most likely chance of success. If your boss asks you to complete that sentence, don't let the opportunity to shape your environment slip by. Learning to truly listen to the conversations was the greatest lesson.

....

ACTIVITY: LISTENING PART 1

1. Starting condition: if you are doing this in a group, have people pair up. If you are working through this workbook alone, find a friend or colleague who will do this exercise with you.

2. Take turns telling a story to your partner. The person sharing should take thirty seconds and tell their partner about something important that they are currently experiencing. The "listener" should completely ignore the storyteller. They should look at their phone, count ceiling tiles, look out the window, do anything but listen. We want the worst "listening" possible here. Then swap roles.

3. Each person should now come up with a short list of words describing how it felt while you were telling your story: _____

ACTIVITY: LISTENING PART 2

1. Now think about listening in the following way: S.O.S.

- S = stop what you are doing. This means close your notebook, put your phone away, and look at the other person with a relaxed and open body position.
- O = open your ears. This means wipe your mind clean of what you think they "might" say or they "always" say and tune in to what they are actually saying.
- S = show you care, not *tell them* you care, but use words that indicate you understood what they were saying and what they might be feeling.

2. Once again, take turns sharing a story with your partner. The person sharing should take thirty seconds and tell their partner about something important that they are currently experiencing. The "listener" should now listen to the storyteller using S.O.S. They should pay attention and not look at their phone. When the thirty seconds are up, swap roles.

3. Each person should now come up with a short list of words describing how it felt while you were telling your story this time: _____

Lessons from the Listening Activity

- We have conducted this experiment in hundreds of workshops all over the globe and have surveyed over ten thousand people. Almost all of the responses the first time around are very negative words, like *angry, unimportant, frustrated, rude, ignored.* The second time there are very positive words, like *heard, respected, present, loved.*

- No one likes to be ignored, yet this is the result when we don't listen. Then we are surprised when people don't show up to work with full engagement. The problem is us. We made them feel that way.

- If someone wants to talk with you, take time and listen. If you don't have time to give full attention, tell them and schedule a better time.

....

 Next time you talk to your boss about a problem, bring a possible solution as well. Encourage the people working for you to bring solutions when they bring you problems. It doesn't necessarily have to be the solution to the problem they bring, but the rule is "one problem, one solution."

....

Next time someone comes to talk to you, try listening like a leader: Effective listening is not about you. It is about them. It's not hearing every word said. It is making sure that the person talking to you feels heard. Effective listening takes effort! Multitasking and listening are not compatible. Effective listening requires giving our full attention. Giving our full attention is not always easy and it takes practice. Follow the three steps—S.O.S.—to make others feel heard:

Use this video developed with Simon Sinek to further your understanding: https://tinyurl.com/nudge145.

....

RESEARCH PERSPECTIVE

"Act your way to new thinking" is fully consistent with a classic psychology study titled "Saying Is Believing." Higgins and Rholes (1978) found that when participants had no reason to feel favorably or unfavorably about someone, but were primed to write a favorable or unfavorable statement about them, they believed what they wrote later on. Further, with a longer delay, participants believed in what they wrote even more! In other words, the act of writing something positive made them feel positive about somebody while the act of writing something negative made them feel negative about somebody, even though it was completely arbitrary whether they were asked to write positive or negative statements.

E. Tory Higgins and William S. Rholes, "'Saying Is Believing': Effects of Message Modification on Memory and Liking for the Person Described," *Journal of Experimental Social Psychology* 14, no. 4 (1978): 363–78.

....

Chapter 10

Short, Early Conversations
Make Efficient Work

A supervisor's conversations with her or his people do not have to consist of telling them what to do. These talks instead become opportunities for your people to get early feedback on how they are tackling problems. This allows them to retain control of the solution. These early, quick discussions will also provide clarity to your people about what you want to accomplish. They do not have to last more than thirty seconds, but they can save hours of wasted time.

....

CHIEF'S PERSPECTIVE

The most difficult aspect of this practice was the fear that I would waste my boss's time, or worse, that he would come up with some new great idea that would completely change the scope of the project I was working on. The reality for me was the short, early conversations prevented rework and corrective work after I thought I was done. Did we get some new ideas? Absolutely! The greatest benefit for me was my boss had insight now on some of the challenges our work entailed. When having these short, early conversations with my team, it helped me help them anticipate potential roadblocks and speed bumps. I remember my team telling me on more than one occasion that I didn't know how hard something was for them. The truth is I had progressed through their same challenges and struggles. These conversations served two purposes. One, they offered me an opportunity to help them. Two, they kept me connected to the challenges that I no longer dealt with as the chief.

....

We implemented this practice after preparation of navigational charts that were perfect but irrelevant (pages 73–75).

QUESTIONS

How would you counter any reluctance on the part of your team to have early, quick discussions with you, the boss, to make sure projects are on course?

_____

_____

_____

_____

_____

_____

_____

Is your staff spending time and money creating flawless charts and reports that are, simultaneously, irrelevant? If so, provide an example.

_____

_____

_____

_____

_____

What can you do in your organization to add "a little rudder far from the rocks" to prevent needing "a lot of rudder next to the rocks"?

_____

_____

_____

_____

_____

What commonplace facts can you leverage to make information more valuable and accessible to your employees?

_____

_____

_____

_____

_____

_____

Think of an example of a practice or procedure that occurs on a regular basis because it has always been done a certain way. Then think of an example of a practice or procedure that occurs regularly out of convenience. Detail them here.

_____

_____

_____

_____

_____

MECHANISM: REPLACE LONG MEETINGS WITH MANY SHORT CONVERSATIONS

DON'T YOU TRUST ME?

One problem that came up as we spread the idea of these short interactions earlier in the process was the question of trust. I could hear the petty officers complaining that the command "didn't trust them," and sometimes they challenged me directly with that complaint. For a long time this bothered me because I actually did trust them, but I didn't know how to answer the question. Then I realized that we were talking about two totally different things.

Short, Early Conversations Make Efficient Work

Trust means this: when you report that we should position the ship in a certain position, *you believe* we should position the ship as you indicated, that it's in the best interest of the organization to do so.

Not trusting you would mean that I thought you might be saying one thing while actually believing something else. Trust is purely a characteristic of the human relationship. Now, whether the position you indicate is *actually* the best tactical position for the *Santa Fe* is a totally different issue, one of physics, time, distance, and the movements of the enemy. These are characteristics of the physical world and have nothing to do with trust.

Trusting people does not mean you have to agree with them. Not agreeing with people does not mean you do not trust them.

Trust is built from transparency over time. How much time depends upon the situation. In an intense life-and-death experience trust (or erosion of trust) can happen very quickly. The more diffuse and diluted the interactions are, in general, the longer it will take for trust to build. Transparency is required of both parties. Leaders are transparent when they think aloud, saying what they are contemplating and why they are making certain decisions. Employees are transparent when they update their leaders on how projects are going, reporting the bad as well as the good, and what decisions they are making.

We see businesses trying to keep all kinds of secrets. Some secrets are legally required, like, for example, a plan to purchase another company, or inside information about contracts, clients, and sales that may materially affect the price of the stock. However, we usually see many more secrets and some are inadvertent. For example, the tiers in the hierarchy, who was at each level, and how one got promoted to the next level up. This is a particularly bad thing not to reveal because humans want to know where they stand in the hierarchy and how they can move upward. As another example, plans to permanently shut down a factory are hidden until the last minute. This results in dysfunctional behavior because the factory could defer all maintenance on the machines, knowing the machines will be decommissioned. Supervisors fear that key people will leave prior to the go-dark day, affecting production. But, then, how do those supervisors feel when they tell their staff that they have a week till they are out of a job? And how do the employees feel?

ACTIVITY: TRANSPARENCY ACTIVITY

On a whiteboard or flip chart, make a vertical line. Label one side "can do now" and on the other side "can do later."

On the "can do now" side, work in small groups to come up with a list of areas where you could be more transparent without any change of policy or law.

On the "can do later" side, list areas where you could be more transparent after changing a policy or law.

Have the groups share their lists.

Pick one item on the "can do now" side and commit to being more transparent there.

Revisit the process in a month.

When we run this activity, groups come up with lists like:

CAN DO NOW	CAN DO LATER
Planned product changes	Takeover plans
Performance evaluations	Pay information
Risks to the business	
Investigations into errors	

Short, Early Conversations Make Efficient Work

To what degree is trust present in your organization? What do you see and hear illustrating that the environment you work in is either highly trusting or not very trusting?

_____

_____

_____

_____

_____

_____

....

Walk around your workplace and ask a team member how a specific project is going. Unless he specifically asks for help, thank him for the update and resist the urge to provide additional instruction.

If you are working as a team member in your organization, take time to let your boss know how you are progressing. Keep them informed of the challenges and successes.

Repeat daily.

....

Chapter 11

Use "I Intend to . . ." to Create
Leaders at Every Level

When we give people instructions, we create dependence. When we give people intent, we create independence. The key to your team becoming more proactive rests in the language the subordinates and superiors use. Sometimes we call this empowerment, but I don't believe we empower people. They are already empowered. What we do is give them the authority to exercise their natural empowerment. Whatever you decide to call it, the way you get there is not by giving people speeches, but by giving people a tool they can use to make decisions at a higher level than they could before.

"Disempowered phrases" that passive followers use:

- We've always done it this way.
- I was told . . . (or "They told me . . .")
- What would you like me to do . . . ?

- What should I do about . . . ?
- Do you think we should . . . ?
- Tell me what to do.

"Empowered phrases" that active leaders use:

- I intend to . . .
- I would like to . . .
- I plan to . . .
- I will . . .
- Let me give you an update.
- Here's what we are thinking about this.

Instead of waiting for an order for the next steps to take, an empowered employee briefly reports to his manager with sufficiently complete information and rationale for the action he intends to take. The employee uses empowered phrases such as "I intend to . . ." to communicate to his manager, who then must act if he or she wishes to stop the employee. In the case of no prohibition or no response, the employee then acts according to their plan. This process of employees thinking out loud as to what they intend to do and why invites them to think at the next higher level, thereby turning the management structure upside down. The use of empowering language builds energetic, emotionally committed employees who think about what needs to be done and the right way to do it.

 The process behind how "I intend to . . ." came into being and how it worked on the *Santa Fe* (pages 81–82).

MECHANISM: USE "I INTEND TO . . ." TO TURN PASSIVE FOLLOWERS INTO ACTIVE LEADERS

QUESTIONS

What do you believe causes us to take control when we should be giving control?

_____

_____

_____

_____

_____

_____

_____

Can you recall a recent incident where your subordinate followed your order because he or she thought you harbored secret information "for executives only"? If you can, please describe the incident.

_____

_____

_____

_____

_____

_____

_____

What would be the most challenging obstacles to implementing "I intend to . . ." in your place of business?

_____

_____

_____

_____

_____

Could your mid-level managers think through and defend their plan of action for the company's next big project? In what ways do you currently prepare them to do so, and in what ways could you better prepare them?

_____

_____

_____

_____

_____

THE LADDER OF LEADERSHIP

Here's a framework for thinking about creating Intent-Based organizations: move people up the Ladder of Leadership. The result will be greater engagement, passion, and involvement.

Use "I Intend to . . ." to Create Leaders at Every Level

Ladder of Leadership

LEVEL	WORKER SAYS	BOSS SAYS
7	I've been doing . . .	What have you been doing?
6	I've done . . .	What have you done?
5	I intend to . . .	What do you intend to do?
4	I would like to . . .	What would you like to do?
3	I think . . .	What do you think?
2	I see . . .	What do you see? Tell me more.
1	Tell me what to do.	I'll tell you what to do.

We use the words "boss" and "worker" simply to denote a hierarchy. The words could be "parent" and "child," "doctor" and "nurse," "teacher" and "student," "pilot" and "copilot," or any hierarchical relationship. Yet the ladder is more than a hierarchy of delegation coded by the language we use at the various levels. At the bottom, we have gofer task-by-task instructions. At the top, we have high autonomy and authority individuals reporting back broadly to their superiors what they have been doing. Here, the employees are not just being given tasks to accomplish, they are determining what should be done. The value of the ladder is that it takes an intangible like "empowerment" and makes it observable and measurable and gives us the words to practice it. Additionally, since it is laid out in small discrete steps, it can be implemented incrementally, which helps both boss and worker have a feeling of safety.

Let's go into those levels in more detail.

At the bottom we have Level 1, where bosses tell workers what to do. When the employee asks, the boss tells them, or maybe the boss doesn't even wait for the employee to ask and they go around telling people what to do. This is classic "know all—tell all" leadership. Employees walk into the boss's office with a problem and ask to be told what to do. Sometimes this is explicit, sometimes implied. They want the boss to do the thinking and take responsibility for the decision. We have surveyed over one hundred groups in conferences and seminars and the biggest reason groups report that workers operate at Level 1 is fear.

At Level 2, "I see," bosses invite workers to Level 2 with words like "what do you see?," "tell me more," "tell me about that," or "what do you see here?" Bosses avoid telling workers what to do, even if it's just for thirty seconds, and play the next level up.

Employees at this level are doing more than simply asking to be told what to do. They are reporting what they are seeing or experiencing. This may be a reaction from a client, a response from a machine, or a change in the competitive landscape. Reporting what we see and simply describing a situation is psychologically safe. Remember, the number one reason people are stuck at "tell me what to do" is fear, and inviting them to say what they see is a very small, safe step up the ladder.

In all cases, worker-initiated conversations are more powerful than boss-initiated conversations. There's a big difference between an employee going to their boss and reporting some new situation and the boss walking around asking questions and probing employees to see what's new.

At Level 3, "What do you think," bosses invite their teams to start sharing their thoughts about cause and effect and sharing possible responses by the organization. This involves more psychological risk than simply description because there's a possibility they might be wrong. Bosses at this level try not to force dichotomous choices but invite the worker to respond probabilistically—with the use of "how." For example, not asking "are you sure?" but "how sure are you?" and not asking "do you support this?" but "how strongly do you support this?" Asking these questions in a probabilistic way makes it easier for workers to respond. The result is greater participation in the response and a wider, more nuanced thinking.

Employees at this level are taking more psychological risk by postulating cause or mulling over possible responses. Often these can be stated as probabilities, such as "I think there's a 60 percent chance that the bearings are going bad." They go beyond simply stating that the machine is vibrating more than normal and offer a cause based upon their interpretation of the data and experience.

At Level 4, "What would you like to do?" bosses invite their team members not only to postulate cause but also to recommend actions to be taken. Again, since these recommendations may become decisions that could later be evaluated, there's a higher level of psychological risk than simply stating observations and postulating cause.

Workers at Level 4 don't quite own the problem, but they are doing better than simply bringing problems to the boss—they are bringing solutions as well.

Level 5, "intent," is my favorite level. It is my favorite level because it invites a high level of communication and it feels to the workers that they have a high level of control. It is the sweet spot of communication and control. With intent, bosses ask "what do you intend to do?" and the team states their intentions.

Intent is powerful for a number of reasons. First, there's a high degree of psychological ownership with intent. Intent is initiated by the subordinate, the worker. Since they initiate it, they own it. In order to tell your boss what you intend to do, there's a natural proactivity that follows. Another powerful aspect of intent is that it invites workers to think like their boss, or think like their boss's boss. It's the activation of this thinking that makes teams operating with intent so effective. Finally, in an Intent-Based organization there's a strong bias toward action. Most organizations are run as permission-based organizations, where it takes a positive affirmation from a boss to approve actions. This creates a system of waiting for e-mail response or pestering the executive assistant to get on the boss's calendar. In Intent-Based organizations, workers give their boss fair warning about an intended action and the rationale. They state 1) why the action is technically correct and safe, and 2) why it aligns with the goals of the organization. In this case, the boss need only nod, but if there is no response from the boss after a set deadline (by default we use twenty-four hours), the action happens. It's this bias for action that allows Intent-Based organizations to run circles around permission-based organizations.

It is desirable to move up the ladder. Giving people more say in decisions invites them to be thoughtful. This in turn increases involvement, engagement, ownership, ultimately, productivity.

But there are conditions that need to be in place in order to move up the ladder. These conditions are the things we talk about, the "But that won't work because . . ." things that come up when we consider moving people up the ladder. To operate at the top of the ladder requires high levels of competence, clarity, trust, planning, authority, and autonomy as well as courage on the part of the leader to divest control to this extent.

There are several natural forces that push organizations toward the bottom of the ladder. First, if you optimize your decisions for the short term, you will always end up at the bottom of the ladder. For any individual instance, it is always faster and easier to "do it yourself" or just tell someone exactly what they need to do. This is where our natural instincts take us. It takes energy and deliberate action to bias for the long term to move up the ladder. However, once you do, the results are tremendous.

Second, under conditions of stress, time pressure, inadequate sleep, or fatigue, the tendency for both leader and worker will be to drop down the ladder.

Finally, in low-trust environments where the blame game is prevalent, there will be a strong gravitational force to pull people toward the bottom of the ladder.

On board the USS *Santa Fe,* junior sailors who were previously told what to do were now asked what they thought. Officers who previously requested permission for operations now stated their intentions. Oversight meetings and checklists were canceled. The result was an explosion of thinking, passion, and engagement; the enduring success of the ship; and the long-term professional advancement of the men. The ship set records in both performance and in retaining people in the Navy, a measure of morale.

ACTIVITY: LADDER OF LEADERSHIP (PART 1)

This is done best in groups of three to five.

1. Draft a short decision-making scenario from work or use one from the Ladder of Leadership card set.* In your scenario identify two actors (boss and worker) and two sides of a decision (choice A or choice B). Here is an example of a scenario.

....

SCENARIO CARD

Parts in this one-thousand-person manufacturing company are normally batch inspected before shipping due to previous quality issues. A batch is late and doing the inspection will result in having to pay express shipping rates.

....

*The Ladder of Leadership card sets can be found at: http://davidmarquet.com/ladder-of
-leadership-cards.

Senior Vice President for Operations: Quality has been a continuing headache for your team.

Production Supervisor: You have received critical feedback because of previous quality issues.

Do you do the quality inspection or not?

....

2. Role-play the scenario. Take turns role-playing the scenario with different people playing the boss and worker. In the workshops we start with "Level 1 boss" and a higher-level worker. When we play out these scenarios the worker comes in with a level of empowerment but gets told what to do by the boss. It's fun to play "bad boss" and say things like "Just do it, you don't get paid to think."

LADDER OF LEADERSHIP ACTIVITY (PART 1):
BASIC DISCUSSION POINTS

A. How does it feel different when the boss is higher than the worker?

B. What difference does it make who speaks first?

ACTIVITY: LADDER OF LEADERSHIP (PART 2)

A. Take-home assignment: over a twenty-four-hour period, have people record and document conversations in the workplace about decisions. The point is to be as true as possible to what was actually said, with minor simplification if needed:

Use "I Intend to . . ." to Create Leaders at Every Level

Boss (title):	Worker (title):												
Decision to Be Made													
Boss Said							Worker Said						
Boss Level							Worker Level						
1	2	3	4	5	6	7	1	2	3	4	5	6	7
Thoughts													

B. Upon reconvening, allow ten minutes for groups to review their conversations with each other and pick one to act out in front of the group. Criteria for selecting the conversation to be acted out are: realistic, recent, relevant, and universally understandable.

C. Now that the groups have picked their conversation to act out, allow five minutes for them to pick two actors and practice the script.

D. In turns, each group sends actors to the front of the room to act out the scenario. They explain the situation and decision to be made and the roles (not the names) of the people they are playing. Then they act out the conversation. They don't say "and then the boss said . . ."; they simply play the role of boss, or worker, and say what they said. Sometimes we videotape these for future training.

E. After listening to the conversation, the group evaluates where the boss and worker were on the ladder and come up with alternate scripting for the boss, worker, or both. In particular, the group looks for ways to rescript the boss's language to invite the worker higher on the ladder in a safe way and rescript the worker's language to enter higher on the ladder.

**LADDER OF LEADERSHIP ACTIVITY (PART 2):
ADVANCED DISCUSSION POINTS**

A. What factors for the worker would cause you to want to operate lower or higher on the ladder?

B. What factors for the boss would cause you to want to operate lower or higher on the ladder?

C. For the worker, how would the previous factors affect where you wanted to operate?

D. For the boss, what were the best strategies for coaxing a worker up the ladder? (See our strategies on the next two pages.)

Notes

_____

_____

_____

_____

_____

_____

_____

For more scenarios, use the Ladder of Leadership cards, and for help writing your own scenarios, go to www.ladderofleadership.com.

👉 The next time one of your employees brings you a decision issue, think about where they are on the Ladder of Leadership and try to invite them to level up.

STRATEGIES FOR INVITING SOMEONE UP THE LADDER

Remember that the reason people are stuck at the bottom is most likely fear, so your job is to make it feel safe for them to move up. Here are things that can help the person feel safe:

- Make the change small. Don't try to push them two or three levels, just invite them to the next level up.
- Give choice. The most basic choice is to move up the ladder or not. Next you could give choices on how they want to respond (by e-mail, verbally), or where (in your office, on

the factory floor), or with whom (by themselves, with co-workers).

- Take responsibility. Make sure they know that the repercussions of a bad decision will fall on you, not them, but that they are helping you by sharing what they think.

....

RESEARCH PERSPECTIVE

"I intend to . . ." creates ownership in goal setting, which gives responsibility to the employee and also increases their commitment to attaining their goals (Locke and Latham, 1990). But intentions can do more than this, too. Peter Gollwitzer has written extensively on intentions. Forming not just goals, but implementation intentions, greatly increases goal attainment. Whereas goal intentions specify a certain end point or desired outcome, implementation intentions "specify the when, where, and how" of reaching the goal. For example: "when situation X arises, I will do Y" (Gollwitzer, 1999).

Edwin A. Locke and Gary P. Latham, *A Theory of Goal Setting and Task Performance* (Englewood Cliffs, NJ: Prentice Hall, 1990).

Peter M. Gollwitzer, "Implementation Intentions: Strong Effects of Simple Plans," *American Psychologist* 54, no. 7 (1999): 493–503.

....

Chapter 12
Return the Problem Unsolved

When we let people solve problems,
they see themselves as part of the solution.

An emergency situation requires quick decisions and clear orders. There may be little time for a discussion with subordinates. However, a vast majority of situations do not require an immediate decision. There is usually time for the team to chew on the situation. With Intent-Based Leadership, you must take time to let others react to the situation as well. You have to create a space for open decision by the entire team, even if that space is only a few minutes, or a few seconds, long. This is harder than in the leader-follower approach because it requires you to anticipate decisions and alert your team to the need for an upcoming one. In a top-down hierarchy, subordinates don't need to be thinking ahead because the boss will make a decision when needed.

How many times do issues that require decisions come up on short

111

notice? If this is happening a lot, you have a reactive organization locked in a downward spiral. When issues aren't foreseen, the team doesn't get time to think about them; a quick decision by the boss is required, which doesn't train the team, and so on.

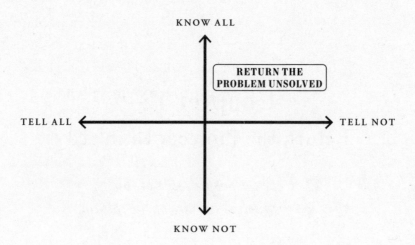

You need to change that cycle. Here are a few ways to get your team thinking for themselves.

- If the decision needs to be made urgently, make it, then explain why, later, when there is time, have the team "red-team" (see page 159) the decision and evaluate it.
- If the decision needs to be made soon, ask for team input, even briefly, then make the decision.
- If the decision can be delayed, then push the decision back to the team to provide input. Do not force the team to come to consensus; that results in whitewashing differences and dissenting votes. Cherish dissent. If everyone thinks like you, you don't need them.

....

CHIEF'S PERSPECTIVE

Returning a problem unsolved can be very difficult, as we are trained and conditioned as leaders to solve problems. The immediate result of having a problem or challenge returned to me was very motivating, especially when there was no urgency on the decision. In the cases where time was critical to the decision, having my boss make a decision and then get the team together after to share his or her insight on how the decision was made helped me develop as a leader. It built a level of competency in our teams that allowed us to solve problems before they actually became problems. Going to the boss with an issue identified and a course of intended action identified helped us shape our future.

....

 By not solving a problem during an exercise for my team, they came up with the solution themselves (pages 89–91).

MECHANISM: RETURN THE PROBLEM UNSOLVED

QUESTIONS

What is the long-term impact of solving your people's problems?

_____

_____

_____

_____

_____

_____

Do you recognize situations in which you need to resist the urge to provide solutions? Give an example.

_____

_____

_____

_____

_____

When problems occur, do you immediately think you just need to manage everything more carefully? In what ways could you start to break away from this type of thinking?

_____

_____

_____

_____

_____

What can you do at your next meeting with senior staff to create a space for open decision making by the entire team?

_____

_____

_____

_____

_____

_____

· ·

👉 The next time one of your employees brings you a problem, return the problem unsolved.

· ·

· ·

RESEARCH PERSPECTIVE

It may sound obvious, but the most important thing for learning is _effort put forth by the learner_ (Halpern and Hakel, 2003). The hidden cost of providing solutions is that we rob people of responsibility, agency, and learning. For a great book on the science of learning, see Bransford et al. (1999), which can be downloaded for free at www.nap.edu.

John D. Bransford, Ann L. Brown, and Rodney R. Cocking, eds., _How People Learn: Brain, Mind, Experience, and School_ (Washington, D.C.: National Academy Press, 1999).

Diane F. Halpern and Milton D. Hakel, "Applying the Science of Learning to the University and Beyond: Teaching for Long-Term Retention and Transfer," _Change: The Magazine of Higher Learning_ 35, no. 4 (2003): 36–41.

· ·

Chapter 13
Eliminate Top-Down Monitoring Systems

Leadership is not for the select few at the top. In highly effective organizations, there are leaders at every level.

Supervisors frequently bemoan the "lack of ownership" in their employees but don't realize that they are taking actions daily that poach ownership from their people. Don't preach and hope for ownership; instead, implement mechanisms that actually give ownership, and eliminate mechanisms that inhibit a sense of ownership. Top-down monitoring systems are very good at destroying any sense of ownership, so the more you can do to eliminate them, the better. I'm not talking about eliminating data collection and measuring processes that simply report conditions without judgment. Those are important as they "make the invisible visible." What you want to avoid are the systems whereby senior personnel are determining what junior personnel should be doing and "holding them accountable."

People work best when accountable to themselves in the broader context of the organization.

When it comes to processes, adherence to the process frequently becomes the objective, as opposed to achieving the objective that the process was put in place to achieve.

In his book *Out of the Crisis,* W. Edwards Deming lays out the leadership principles that became known as TQL, or Total Quality Leadership. Deming explains how efforts to improve the process make the organization more efficient, while efforts to monitor the process make the organization less efficient. Monitoring your employees—"We are checking up on you"—will have a harmful effect on their initiative, vitality, and passion.

The department heads should monitor their own departments and what is due. They should be responsible for their own performance and the performance of their own departments. Their boss should not spend a lot of effort telling them what to do.

 We had an onerous tracking system called "the tickler" that we eliminated with great celebration (pages 94–97).

MECHANISM: ELIMINATE TOP-DOWN MONITORING SYSTEMS

QUESTIONS

In what ways are you underutilizing the ideas, creativity, and passions of your mid-level managers who want to be responsible for their departments' work products? How could you change this?

_____

_____

Eliminate Top-Down Monitoring Systems

_____

_____

_____

_____

_____

Could you turn over your monitoring system to your department heads and rid yourself of meetings in the process? What effect do you think this would have?

_____

_____

_____

_____

_____

_____

What are some of the top-down monitoring systems in play within your organization? How can you work to eliminate them?

_____

_____

_____

_____

_____

_____

THE FOUR LEVELS OF ACCOUNTABILITY SYSTEMS

Level 1: People are not told what they are accountable for and therefore don't do their jobs. This is chaos.

Level 2: People are told what they are accountable for but don't do their jobs because of overwork or focus on the wrong things. This is the most inefficient because there is overhead for telling and monitoring but the work isn't getting done.

Level 3: People know what they are responsible for and do their jobs. There are systems to hold people accountable. It is a compliant system, where people feel like they are being forced into doing their jobs. This is where most organizations strive to be, but this is top-down.

Level 4: People are not told what they are accountable for because they've figured it out on their own, and so they do their jobs anyway. The monitoring system is discarded and the team monitors themselves. This is where we were able to get to after throwing out the monitoring systems. This is a highly energized system, where people are engaged in defining their work and doing it.

In a traditional organization, accountability processes are designed with the idea that you (obviously) can't hold yourself accountable for your work, so your boss needs to do it for you.

In an Intent-Based organization, people hold themselves accountable for their jobs, their work, their performance. The role of the leader in an Intent-Based Leadership organization is not to "hold you accountable" but to help you hold yourself accountable. Sometimes we call these "accountability partners." They can be bosses but more typically are peers and subordinates.

Eliminate Top-Down Monitoring Systems

In a traditional organization, people dread the periodic (weekly? daily?) accountability meeting. In Intent-Based organizations, people ask others, "Can you help me stay on track with my goal?" It's a totally different feeling and one that inspires not only efficiency but also creativity and energy.

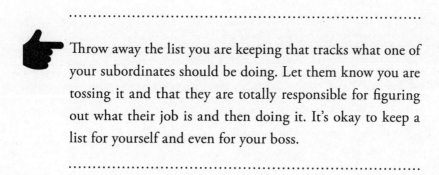

Throw away the list you are keeping that tracks what one of your subordinates should be doing. Let them know you are tossing it and that they are totally responsible for figuring out what their job is and then doing it. It's okay to keep a list for yourself and even for your boss.

Chapter 14
Think Out Loud

When we teach people to think out loud, it helps
avoid silent assumptions, adds transparency, and builds trust.

Thinking out loud is essential for making the leap from leader-follower to Intent-Based Leadership. However, there is a strong cultural bias against thinking out loud in a hierarchical business structure. In order to make the fewest mistakes when reporting on things, subordinates will say as little as possible. If you limit all discussion to crisp orders and eliminate all contextual discussion, you get a pretty quiet place. It takes a team effort to be successful, but in practice it often amounts to a bunch of individuals, each working in their own shells, rather than a rich collaboration.

It is important to invite your entire workforce to say what they are seeing, thinking, believing, feeling skeptical about, fearing, worrying about, and hoping for the future. Make the barrier to stating differences of opinion as low as possible. When you hear what your subordinates are thinking, it makes it much easier for you to keep your mouth shut and let them execute their plans. It is generally when they are quiet and you don't know what they would do next that you are tempted to step in. Cultivate and encourage a constant buzz of discussions among all members of your team. By monitoring the level of buzz, more than the actual content, you can gauge how well the operation is running and whether everyone is sharing information.

The adherence to formal communications unfortunately crowds out less formal but highly important contextual information needed for peak performance. Phrases like "I think . . ." or "I am assuming . . ." or "It is likely . . ." that are not specific and concise orders are examples of the informal communication necessary to make the Intent-Based Leadership model work. You should be comfortable with context-rich conversations that include talking about hunches, gut feelings, or anything with probabilities attached to them.

The issue of communication is for everyone. The boss needs to think out loud with words such as "Here's where we need to be, and here's why." If all you need your people to do is follow orders, it isn't important that they understand what you are trying to accomplish. But we operate in a highly complex world, with the vagaries of an ever-changing environment. It's not enough to point in a direction and hope things come out well. When you as the boss "think out loud," you are in essence imparting context and experience to your subordinates. You are also modeling that lack of certainty is strength and certainty is arrogance.

Having the officer of the deck stating his thoughts and intentions out loud allowed me to stay quiet and let him run the show (pages 102–4).

MECHANISM: THINK OUT LOUD

QUESTIONS

Do you ever walk around your facility listening solely to what is being communicated through informal language? If so, what do you observe?

_____

_____

_____

_____

_____

_____

How comfortable are people in your organization with talking about their hunches and their gut feelings? In what ways is the structure of your environment responsible for this?

_____

_____

_____

_____

_____

_____

What are two specific ways you can create an environment in which people freely express their uncertainties and fears as well as their innovative ideas and hopes?

_____

_____

_____

_____

_____

_____

Are you willing to let your staff see that your lack of certainty is strength and certainty is arrogance? To what degree does trust factor into doing so?

_____

_____

_____

_____

_____

_____

AN EXAMPLE OF PRACTICAL APPLICATION

Teaching my children to drive was a stressful time for me. I would sit on the passenger side of the car while they drove, and I couldn't help but see all the potential dangers (e.g., a family playing in a driveway, an approaching car, a light that was turning red) and point them out. This irritated my kids, who universally responded with exasperation, "I see that." Of course, I didn't know that they saw it.

In response to this situation, we adopted the idea of think out loud. Actually, it was an even more basic variation of think out loud, which was say what you see. With say what you see, they would supply a near-continual monologue that sounded something like this: "I see the family playing in the

Think Out Loud

driveway. They should stay there, but if they come into the road, I am ready to stop. I see the stop sign ahead. I see the car approaching the intersection. I have the right of way and intend to proceed, but if they don't stop, I am ready to stop." With this dialogue going on, I was able to stay quiet.

··

👉 At your next meeting, practice thinking out loud by telling your team your hidden assumptions, fears, and worries about the project. Be vulnerable and set the example with your own behavior.

··

Chapter 15
Embrace the Inspectors

On the *Santa Fe,* we called the idea of being open and inviting outside criticism "embrace the inspectors." It was part of our philosophy of "don't be good, get better." Inspectors for us were generally official Navy auditors, observers, bosses, and inspectors who were assigned to monitor our performance and report to another part of the Navy. You may not have these kinds of inspectors, but you may be getting feedback in other ways. Now I view posted book reviews and surveys of my workshops as my new inspectors.

On the *Santa Fe* we used the inspectors to disseminate our ideas throughout the larger organization, to learn from others, and to document issues to improve our operations. When we embraced the inspectors, we signaled that our team was responsible for our own circumstances and in charge of our own destiny. It helped us avoid a mind-set of victimhood.

Concerning areas where you are doing something exceptionally innovative, you should view the inspectors as advocates with whom to share your good practices.

Concerning areas where you are doing things poorly and need help, you should view them as sources of information and solutions. This creates an atmosphere of learning and curiosity among your people, as opposed to an attitude of defensiveness.

The "red tag violation" incident and how we addressed it demonstrated the importance of embracing the inspector for organizational learning (pages 108–11).

MECHANISM: EMBRACE THE INSPECTORS (ANOTHER WAY OF SAYING THIS IS, "DON'T BE GOOD, GET BETTER!")

QUESTIONS

List and detail several ways that you use outside groups, the public, social media comments, and corporate or government audits to improve your organization.

_____

_____

_____

_____

_____

_____

_____

Embrace the Inspectors

What are some potential costs of being open about problems in your organization, and what are some potential benefits?

_____

_____

_____

_____

_____

_____

How can you leverage the knowledge of the inspectors to make your team smarter?

_____

_____

_____

_____

_____

_____

In what ways can you improve your team's cooperation with those inspectors?

_____

_____

_____

_____

_____

_____

How can you "use" the inspectors to help your organization? List specific ways.

_____

_____

_____

_____

_____

_____

_____

I think the idea of embracing the inspector goes beyond thinking about formal or official outside inspectors. It should include any sort of feedback you can get about how you are doing. The idea is "don't be good, get better." In other words, don't spend any effort defending your reputation or attempting to protect a sense of how good you are. Instead, focus on how you can get better.

··

👉 The next time you receive criticism, feedback, or are being audited, ask questions only to clarify and fully understand what the auditor is telling you. Do not try to defend what you've done or explain it. Just try to learn as much as possible during the interaction.

··

....

RESEARCH PERSPECTIVE

As it turns out, there is a vast amount of scientific evidence in support of this simple point. Perhaps the most relevant concept is Carol Dweck's theory of growth versus fixed mind-sets, which notes that people can have a tendency to approach achievement situations with either an orientation toward learning or an orientation toward performing. When people adopt a learning orientation, a "growth mind-set," they tend to be more resilient, creative, and helpful, and social interactions are less taxing to themselves and others. For more information on this, check out Simon Moss's summary hosted on www.sicotests.com, the goal orientation Wikipedia entry, or Dweck's (1986) *American Psychologist* article.

Carol S. Dweck, "Motivational Processes Affecting Learning," *American Psychologist* 41, no. 10 (1986): 1040–8.

"Goal Orientation." Wikipedia, https://en.wikipedia.org/wiki/Goal_orientation. Accessed on July 20, 2017.

....

PART III
Mechanisms for Competence

One of the pillars that support control is competence. Competence means that people have the intimate technical knowledge necessary to make decisions. The emphasis in this workbook thus far has been on pushing decision making and control to lower and lower levels in the organization. However, control by itself isn't enough.

In addition to a robust and effective training program, the following mechanisms strengthen technical competence:

- Take deliberate action.
- Learn (everywhere, all the time).
- Don't brief, certify.
- Continually and consistently repeat the message.
- Specify goals, not methods.

....

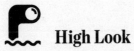 **High Look**

The core of the Intent-Based Leadership system is giving control to employees. The previous part was about different ways we can give control to our team as a leader and empower ourselves as team members.

The issue becomes giving control without allowing chaos. Chaos is bad, especially on a nuclear submarine. There are two main pillars that allow this: technical competence (which is the focus of this next part) and organizational clarity. When divesting control is supported by competence and clarity, the result is distributed decision making and unity of effort.

....

Chapter 16

Take Deliberate Action

When we engage our minds in what we do,
we perform with better results.

The inevitability of mistakes is not an acceptable assumption. The mechanism of taking deliberate action prevents you from making a mistake in the first place by engaging your brain before acting. This means that prior to any action, you pause, vocalize, and gesture toward what you are about to do, and only after taking a deliberate pause do you execute the action. The intent is to eliminate those "automatic" mistakes. Since the goal of "take deliberate action" is to introduce deliberateness in the mind of the person acting, it doesn't matter whether anyone is around. Deliberate actions are not performed for the benefit of an observer or an inspector.

In team settings, an additional benefit occurs when you take deliberate action; as you pause, vocalize, and gesture, it allows your adjacent team members an opportunity to step in and correct mistaken actions before they are taken. If you are in a business where there is an interface between humans and nature (like on a submarine, for example), the concept of taking deliberate action is pretty clear-cut. Additional examples include electric utility companies, airlines and cruise lines, manufacturing plants, and hospitals. In these kinds of organizations, you'll be able to see immediately how acting deliberately would help reduce mistakes. The challenge will be when things are happening quickly, or need to happen quickly, as in a casualty in a power plant or during emergency room procedures in a hospital. Then it's even more important that actions be performed correctly. You don't have time to "undo" something that's wrong.

If your business doesn't have an obvious interface with nature and is more service oriented or intellectual, "take deliberate action" still applies but in a slightly different way. It applies at the moment someone signs a form, authorizes an action, or sends an e-mail.

To implement the mechanism of take deliberate action, management must overcome the perception by their people that the mechanism was for someone else's (a supervisor's or an inspector's) benefit or just a training exercise. Take deliberate action is the single most powerful mechanism your organization can implement for successfully reducing mistakes and achieving operational excellence.

We invented "take deliberate action" to reduce human error (pages 117–21).

MECHANISM: TAKE DELIBERATE ACTION

QUESTIONS

How do you feel and react when an employee admits to doing something on autopilot, without deliberately thinking about the action or

its consequences? Does your reaction to the situation help that employee to not act mindlessly in the future or simply scold in the present?

_____

_____

_____

_____

_____

_____

In what ways could implementing a system of taking deliberate action eliminate errors in your company or within certain departments in your company?

_____

_____

_____

_____

_____

Do you think employees in your workplace will revert to acting hastily and automatically in a real-life situation? If so, explain why you think that they would and what steps you could take to avoid this.

_____

_____

_____

_____
_____
_____

How effectively do you feel you learn from mistakes? How well do you feel your team learns from mistakes? Please provide some examples.

_____
_____
_____
_____
_____
_____

Taking deliberate action is easy to picture in a manufacturing, medical, or an operational setting such as operating a power plant. In these settings we have people taking some physical action. But in "office" settings, the final act of a process is almost always a physical one—uploading a patch to a server, making a phone call to a client, entering the room for a presentation. In these situations as well, deliberate action would be helpful.

 The next time you are about to take a physical action, pause a moment and review in your mind whether it is the right thing to do, whether your hand is on the correct knob or breaker, and whether you are about to move it to the correct position. Bonus points if you vocalize the step you are about to take during this pause.

Hint: You may want to let your coworkers know you are trying something new.

....

Chapter 17
We Learn (Everywhere, All the Time)

Do not divest too much control without first ensuring your organization is competent to handle more decision-making authority. When you delegate authority to make decisions further down the hierarchy, your people's operational and technical knowledge takes on a greater importance. There is an extra burden for operational competence.

If all you need to do is what you are told, then you don't need to understand your craft. However, as your ability to make decisions increases, then you need intimate technical and operational knowledge on which to base those decisions. Control without competence is chaos.

You should look at your training program in a new light. It isn't just an administrative program or a program to minimize errors. It is a "key enabler" to allow you to pass decision-making authority to lower and lower levels in your organization. Want to have a training program that employees will want to go to? Here's how it should work:

The purpose of training is to increase technical and operational knowledge.

The result of increased technical and operational competence is the ability to delegate increased decision making to the employees.

Increased decision making among your employees will naturally result in greater engagement, motivation, and initiative.

You will end up with significantly higher productivity, morale, and effectiveness.

 We developed the USS *Santa Fe* creed to identify our core activity of learning (pp. 126–29).

MECHANISM: WE LEARN (EVERYWHERE, ALL THE TIME)

QUESTIONS

Which areas in your business are marred by mistakes because the lower-level employees don't have enough technical competence to make good decisions?

_____

_____

_____

_____

_____

_____

We Learn (Everywhere, All the Time)

Which areas in your business are marred by mistakes because you don't have enough clarity to make good decisions?

_____

_____

_____

_____

_____

_____

Consider writing a creed for your organization that includes a "we learn" philosophy. How could you implement a "we learn" policy among your junior and senior staff?

_____

_____

_____

_____

_____

_____

Are your people eager to go to training? If not, how could you make them more eager?

_____

_____

_____

_____

_____

_____

_____

ACTIVITY: CREATING A TRAINING PROGRAM TO SUPPORT DECISION MAKING

At your next leadership meeting, try the following activity:

1.   Hand out a bunch of index cards and markers.

2.   Start with this sentence completion: Our company would be more effective if [level] management could make decisions about [subject]. You specify the level of the organization but ask the group to fill in the subjects.

3.   Once you have the set of cards, post them on the wall and go on break. Let people mill around looking at what they've written.

4.   Down-select to a couple of subjects.

5.   Ask the question: What, technically, do the people at this level of the organization need to know in order to make that decision?

6.   Again, answer on the cards, post them, and go on break.

Now you'll have a relevant list of topics for training, and you can directly connect the training topics to increased employee decision making and control—in a word, empowerment. When you set up the training, don't forget to communicate this thought process to the group. That way they'll know why they are going to attend training and want to attend, knowing it's their path to greater decision-making authority.

A key philosophy of "we learn" is that you learn as much as possible from the things you are already doing. We found that if we just paid attention to our everyday operations, like starting the reactor, getting under way, and submerging the ship, we could learn a lot.

There is a great program that the nuclear Navy called "theory to practice" that does just this. With theory to practice we would think about an operation we were about to do and plan it theoretically first. Say we were practicing ventilating the ship, which is when we come to periscope depth and raise a mast above the surface. We start a blower and replace the stale air with fresh air.

The measure of performance for how fast you are refreshing the air is called the half-life. It's the length of time it takes to change half the air in the submarine. You can calculate a theoretical half-life based on the volume of air and the capacity of the blower, but that's what should happen "in theory." When you actually ventilate the ship, you can measure the half-life by plotting the concentration of a contaminant in the air. When we would ventilate, we would go through the theoretical calculation, assign a person to take extra data on the concentration of contaminants, and then calculate the actual half-life, which measured how fast we were refreshing the air. Not only did this solidify the connection between what we'd studied in school and the physical characteristics of operating the submarine, but it allowed us to detect problems early. If, for example, the actual half-life was less than the theoretical half-life, we would see a problem with the blower capacity or an obstruction in a pipe that we would want to solve.

....

 As an employee, the next time you have an onerous, tedious task, ask yourself what you can learn from doing it. Think about that as you perform the task.

As a boss, the next time one of your employees comes to you to report a problem, ask him or her "What did we learn?"

....

....

RESEARCH PERSPECTIVE

Are you, your coworkers, or your employees so busy getting things done that there's no time to focus on learning? The good news is that the scientific literature shows this is largely a mind-set (Dweck, 1986), and that goal attainment is most likely to happen when people frame their intentions as learning goals (a growth mind-set), as opposed to performance goals (Gollwitzer, 1999). But if they must be performance goals, frame them as promotion goals (what you want to accomplish), not prevention goals (what you want to avoid) (Higgins, 1997).

Carol S. Dweck, "Motivational Processes Affecting Learning," *American Psychologist* 41, no. 10 (1986): 1040–8.

Peter M. Gollwitzer, "Implementation Intentions: Strong Effects of Simple Plans," American Psychologist 54, no. 7 (1999): 493–503.

E. Tory Higgins, "Beyond Pleasure and Pain," *American Psychologist* 52, no. 12 (1997): 1280–1300.

....

Chapter 18
Don't Brief, Certify

A briefing is a passive activity for everyone except the briefer. Everyone else is "briefed." There is no responsibility for preparation or study. It's easy to just nod and say "Ready" without full intellectual engagement. Furthermore, the sole responsibility in participating in a brief is to show up. A brief, as such, is not a decision point. The operation is going to happen, and we are simply talking about it first.

A certification is different from a brief in that, during a certification, the person in charge of the team asks questions. At the end of the certification, a decision is made as to whether the team is ready to perform the upcoming operation. If the team has not adequately demonstrated the necessary knowledge during the certification, the operation should be postponed. Certifications shift the onus of preparation onto the participants. All participants are active. The change from passive briefs to active certifications will change your people's behavior. When people know they will be asked questions, they study their responsibilities ahead of time. This increases their intellectual involvement significantly. People are thinking about what they will be required to do and independently study for it.

An effective survey question to ask your employees is how many minutes a week they spend learning on their own—not mandated, not directed. Typically, it's a small number. An organizational measure of improving health would be to increase that number. If you want engaged teams, don't brief, certify!

....

CHIEF'S PERSPECTIVE

Learning to use the certification process was a challenging first step for many. We have conditioned workers to come to work and do what they are told. The level of engagement in that environment is woefully insufficient. Shifting from the "tell me what to do" mind-set to a proactive mind-set takes work, but the rewards are amazing. It leads to having more control over your work. Briefing my teams put all of the responsibility on me. Participating in a brief as a team member was just as draining. When we shifted to certifications, the challenge of knowing that I was going to talk about my role in the process helped me to learn the big picture. Knowing how my actions and concerns impacted others made me a better team player. Hearing from others during a certification provided that same value to me. It reinforced the idea that together we are much better than each individual. The certification process highlighted how easy it is to miss important aspects when one person is responsible for telling/briefing the team on what needed to be done. Additionally, a secondary benefit to the certification process was the opportunity to display my competence and clarity to the boss. As a team leader I also saw my team's competence and clarity.

....

The "best practice" of briefing is only a best practice if you want people to do what they are told. See how we discovered this when submerging the submarine (pages 135–38).

MECHANISM: DON'T BRIEF, CERTIFY

QUESTIONS

In what ways could you shift responsibility for performance from the briefer to the participants?

_____

_____

_____

_____

_____

_____

How much preparation do your people do prior to attending an event or operation? How could you encourage more preparation?

_____

_____

_____

_____

_____

_____

_____

When was the last time you had a briefing on a project? What behavior did you see from the listeners? How engaged were they or did they tune out the procedures? Explain the behavior and attitude of the listeners in your last briefing, including positive behaviors of engagement and negative behaviors of absentness.

_____

_____

_____

_____

_____

_____

What would it take to start certifying that your project teams know what the goals are and how they are to contribute to them?

_____

_____

_____

_____

_____

_____

Don't Brief, Certify

In what ways can you assume more responsibility within the Intent-Based Leadership model? Identify what near-term events will be accomplished and the role each team member will fulfill. Outline a plan.

_____

_____

_____

_____

_____

_____

I believe the idea of don't brief, certify works because it fundamentally shifts responsibility from the boss to the people in the organization for their level of knowledge. On the Ladder of Leadership, it is the equivalent of moving from "Tell me what to do" to "I think" for the workers. It also spurs leaders to think because they need to make a deliberate decision about whether they are ready to proceed with an operation rather than simply doing what's next on the schedule.

....

 Plan a certification! Look ahead on your calendar and select an event for which you might normally do a brief, and plan a certification instead. Work with your team so that they know you will be asking them questions during the certification. When done, make a deliberate decision whether you are ready to commence the event. Example events include:

- Sailors submerging the submarine
- Doctors and nurses performing a medical procedure

153

- Pilots starting an airplane flight
- A project team meeting with a client
- A restaurant crew starting the restaurant shift
- A manufacturing team starting the manufacturing shift
- A maintenance department commencing maintenance on a piece of equipment
- A cruise ship operational team getting a cruise ship under way
- Teachers and administrators starting the school year
- A software team releasing an update, feature, or patch
- A batter preparing to walk to the batting box

....

....

RESEARCH PERSPECTIVE

You may have heard the adage, "I hear and I forget. I see and I remember. I do and I understand." This basic premise is at the heart of "Active Learning," a teaching strategy that engages students in the learning process and increases retention (Prince, 2004). The goal of any training or education effort is to apply what gets learned during training to the work environment (Halpern and Hakel, 2003). This is called transfer of training. The most important consideration for long-term retention and transfer of knowledge is "practice at retrieval," which strengthens the memory trace. When we passively take in information, there is no practice at retrieval. By contrast, when we are asked to produce information, we strengthen our memory and ability to apply what we know. This is why it is much better for people to be actively engaged in a learning activity, like a certification, than to be passive consumers of a lecture or briefing.

Diane F. Halpern and Milton D. Hakel, "Applying the Science of Learning to the University and Beyond: Teaching for Long-Term Retention and Transfer," *Change: The Magazine of Higher Learning* 35, no. 4 (2003): 36–41.

Michael Prince, "Does Active Learning Work? A Review of the Research," *Journal of Engineering Education* 93, no. 3 (2004): 223–31.

....

Chapter 19
Continually and Consistently
Repeat the Message

When you are guiding your people to change to an Intent-Based Leadership organization, you must have a relentless, consistent repetition of your new direction for decision-making behavior: repeating the same message day after day, meeting after meeting, event after event. Sounds redundant, repetitive, and boring, but what's the alternative? Changing the message? That results in confusion and a lack of direction. Old habits die hard, even when people are emotionally on board with the change.

I had an advantage on board the *Santa Fe* that you probably won't have: my people couldn't leave, and we worked on a twenty-four-hour basis. I had many opportunities every day, at meals, training events, and real operations, to reinforce the behaviors we wanted. This accelerated the adoption of the new habits.

When you bring in something new, something that has never been seen before, you can talk about it and some will adopt it quickly; others will take longer. When you explain a change to your people, they hear and think they know what you mean, but they don't. They might not have ever had a picture of what you are talking about. They can't see in their imagination how it works. They are not being intentionally deceitful; they just are not picturing what you are picturing.

Moreover, if they understand what you mean, they might be skeptical that this new way of doing business, which is different from anything they've seen before, could be better. How is it possible to be in an organization for so many years and not have seen this?

Example: I had been talking about taking care of our people, but it wasn't until I made a rule that no watch stander could have a better rotation than the one below him did that my leaders truly understood what I meant.

....

CHIEF'S PERSPECTIVE

This concept was critical to implement and sustain change. Oftentimes when we get a great idea or vision, especially one that is contrary to years of conditioning, conveying the idea is the most difficult aspect. We feel like sharing information and ideas is enough to convey our vision, but the truth is unless your whole team was involved in the conceptualization, the "whys" behind the change, they find it more comfortable to do "what we have always done." I cannot number the times my team told me they were doing something because that is the way it had always been done, even when they thought they had a better way to accomplish the same task. Continually and consistently repeating the message helped the concept sink in and become habit. I also found myself, at times, starting to default to the way we had always done things, but because leadership was continually and consistently repeating the message, it was easier to successfully execute change.

....

The story of Sled Dog showed the importance of continually and consistently repeating the message (pages 142–50).

MECHANISM: CONTINUALLY AND CONSISTENTLY REPEAT THE MESSAGE

QUESTIONS

What are some techniques you can use to remind yourself to repeat a consistent message over and over, without getting frustrated?

_____

_____

_____

_____

_____

_____

What issues do you anticipate you will encounter while you try to repeat your new message to your employees?

_____

_____

_____

_____

_____

_____

_____

What messages do you need to keep repeating in your business to make sure your management team doesn't take care of themselves first, to the neglect of their team?

_____

_____

_____

_____

_____

_____

What messages do you wish leadership was repeating in your organization?

_____

_____

_____

_____

_____

_____

I think that consistently repeating the message is definitely necessary but is not sufficient to cause organizational change. Where the changes were defined precisely as language changes (say "I intend to . . ." instead of "I request permission to . . ."), then this repetition worked. However, where the changes were defined as cultural norms (we take care of our people on the *Santa Fe*), then repeating the message was insufficient to cause the change. It wasn't until I made a rule such as the "no better than" rule for watch rotation that my crew understood what I meant and changed.

The idea that repeating the message isn't enough supports the mechanism of "act your way to new thinking, don't think your way to new action." My point of this chapter is that leaders should not get frustrated when they find it necessary to repeat a message, nor should they change the message frequently. If you do, you will sabotage any chance of moving your organization forward.

....

CHIEF'S PERSPECTIVE

The adoption of certain rules and actions to help facilitate change was critical in improving the culture in our organization. Critical to the process was the idea of having the team generate the ideas for the rules that they thought would help facilitate the change.

....

....

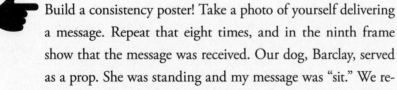 Build a consistency poster! Take a photo of yourself delivering a message. Repeat that eight times, and in the ninth frame show that the message was received. Our dog, Barclay, served as a prop. She was standing and my message was "sit." We repeated that eight times. In the ninth frame, Barclay was sitting and I said, "Good dog." The point is not to say, "Dammit . . ." after the third or fourth repetition of the message.

....

Chapter 20
Specify Goals, Not Methods

Provide your people with the objective and let them figure out the method. Once you free them from following a prescribed way of doing things, they will be motivated to come up with ingenious ways to best accomplish the goal. You want to avoid an unwavering compliance with procedures that have the tendency to supplant the objective as the ultimate goal. Although we don't want people to founder and we want adherence to procedures and best practices, we nevertheless should be on guard against this tendency.

Picture a box of LEGOs, the building blocks. I thought of things like starting up the reactor, submerging the ship, and other technical aspects of running the submarine as LEGOs.

Now imagine some of the wild LEGO creations you've seen—all the interesting and creative things that people have made when assembling LEGOs. This is where you want the experimentation to happen. Each step on the way to performing the final task was one building block: how we talked to each other, how we treated each other, how we did our operational planning.

We found it useful to be clear on differentiating between procedures we wanted strict compliance on (such as starting up the reactor) and procedures we wanted innovation on (such as putting out a fire). I call this the LEGOs rule. The LEGOs are the individual building blocks, and they should not be broken. This is not where we are looking for innovation. We are looking for compliance. Typically, the LEGO blocks consisted of man-versus-nature issues like operating machinery, running the reactor, driving the ship through the ocean. On the other hand, some processes were more like assembling LEGOs. Here we wanted creativity and innovation. These tended to be issues that could be characterized as man versus man—issues about how we talked with each other, how we organized ourselves for an operation, how we conducted training.

....

CHIEF'S PERSPECTIVE

Knowing the difference between operations that require compliance and operations that will excel with creativity and innovation comes from building one's technical competence and clarity. As I developed my skill sets, I remember learning the theory behind the things that we did. As I mastered the theory and could start adjusting parameters, I learned how I could innovate and create to improve things. I also learned the areas that required strict compliance. No matter how much I thought about doing things differently, ensuring safety always required compliance to a process or procedure. I could not propose adjusting a procedure if I did not understand the entire challenge. This only comes from a thorough understanding of the issue at hand.

....

Specify Goals, Not Methods

We changed our way of practicing fire drills so that they emphasized and rewarded prompt application of fire extinguishers and hoses to the fire as opposed to following the prescribed role (pages 153–57).

MECHANISM: SPECIFY GOALS, NOT METHODS

QUESTIONS

In what ways do your processes control you rather than help you? How could you remedy this?

_____

_____

_____

_____

_____

_____

How could you ensure adherence to procedure while at the same time ensuring that accomplishing the objective remains foremost in everyone's mind? Detail a plan.

_____

_____

_____

_____

_____

Have you reviewed your operations manual lately to replace general terminology with clear, concise, specific directions? What could you change?

_____

_____

_____

_____

_____

_____

_____

In what ways is your staff complying with procedures to the neglect of accomplishing the company's overall objectives? What are some of your ideas on how to remedy this?

_____

_____

_____

_____

_____

_____

Another way to think about this issue is to understand your relationship with variability. Essentially, the history of the industrial revolution has been a history of a war on variability. Starting with individual craftsmen where each individual product differed and moving to guilds with common training and practices, to industrialization, assembly lines, up through Deming's Total Quality Leadership and Lean Six Sigma programs, all have sought to reduce variability (or diversity).

Specify Goals, Not Methods

The problem is that while reducing variability is what wins for manufacturing, increasing variability (or diversity) is what wins for thinking. It's therefore the leader's job to identify whether a certain process will win by reducing variability or by increasing variability and to apply the appropriate rules.

 Get a box of LEGOs. Have an activity with your team where they are to build something, say a car or a building. For some teams, simply tell them to build the object. Provide basic requirements, such as "it must be able to stand on its own." For other teams, specify in as minute detail as possible exactly what to do, without telling them what it is. For example, provide instructions such as "Line four white eight-bump LEGOs end to end. On top of those, attach four four-bump LEGOs, overlapping the eight-bump LEGOs."

Debrief as a group. Observe and discuss the differences in the structures. Discuss how it felt to be part of each team.

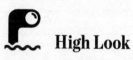 High Look

We have now completed the section on looking anew at leadership (which was an encouragement to think of leadership as giving control and creating leaders rather than taking control and making followers). We also went through the part on giving control and how it's done. Giving control operates on two levels. At the personal level, we give control by moving the people we interact with up the Ladder of

Leadership. It's something everyone can do simply by changing his or her language. At the organizational level, we give control by changing policy documents (pushing authority to information) to give people lower in the organization more decision-making authority. Remember, this is not empowering them, for they are already empowered. It means giving them the language and tools to exercise their natural empowerment. The two supporting pillars when giving control and achieving unity of effort with distributed decision making are technical competence and organizational clarity. We just completed the competence part, and the clarity part comes next.

....

PART IV
Mechanisms for Clarity

As more decision-making authority is pushed down the chain of command, it becomes increasingly important that everyone throughout the organization understands what the organization is about. This is called clarity, and it is the second supporting leg (along with competence) that is needed in order to distribute control.

Clarity means people at all levels of an organization clearly and completely understand what the organization is about. This is needed because people in the organization can make decisions against a set of criteria that includes what the organization is trying to accomplish. If clarity of purpose is misunderstood, then the criteria by which a decision is made will be skewed, and suboptimal decisions will be made.

The book to read is Simon Sinek's *Start with Why*.

The following are mechanisms for clarity:

- Take care of your people and build trust.
- Use your legacy for clarity.
- Use guiding principles for decision criteria.
- Immediately reward desired behaviors.
- Begin with the end in mind.
- Encourage a questioning attitude over blind obedience.

Chapter 21
Take Care of Your People and Build Trust

*If you take care of your people,
your people will take care of your business.*

It's hard to find a leadership book that doesn't encourage you to "take care of your people." However, taking care of your people does not mean protecting them from the consequences of their own behavior. That's the path to irresponsibility. What it does mean is giving them every available tool and advantage to achieve their aims in life, beyond the specifics of the job.

I reported in chapter 19, "Continually and Consistently Repeat the Message," how even that wasn't enough to change organizational culture. We needed to implement a rule that no senior watch stander could have a better rotation than a junior watch stander. It was only after living with this rule that everyone on board understood what this meant and only then that visitors coming to the *Santa Fe* expressed wonder at the culture we had created. Several of the officers who went on to command their own submarines adopted this same practice.

Remember, trust is not about having the right answer; it means we are on the same team and have common objectives. For the leader, this means being zealously dedicated to improving the lives of your people. For employees, this means having the interests of the organization foremost in mind when making decisions.

....

CHIEF'S PERSPECTIVE

This can be a difficult challenge for many. Oftentimes people will assume some extreme behavior modification is associated with this idea of "taking care of your people." In the role of chief, I had to work hard to ensure that I wasn't operating in a realm of extremes. Taking care of my people had to mean that I was helping them develop their expertise, and I was holding them accountable for their responsibilities. The chief did have the role of disciplinarian with the young sailors and it was very easy to default toward the strictest form of punishment when we needed to allow them to suffer the consequences of their choices. One thought that helped me was to remember that no one on my team joined the Navy with the idea of making as many bad choices as they possibly could. It is the same in any organization. People do not join an organization because they don't want to succeed. Taking care of me meant challenging me to push myself, to expand my knowledge, and to increase my control over my work. Having conversations about that limit helped keep things in check, but what I found most often was that I was way more capable than I imagined I could be. Because I was challenged and the challenges were tempered with feedback and mentoring, my skills and expertise were greatly expanded. Additionally, the trust between me and my superiors grew exponentially.

....

 We changed our training process to assist our sailors in getting promoted (pages 166–69).

MECHANISM: TAKE CARE OF YOUR PEOPLE AND BUILD TRUST

QUESTIONS

What do you see in terms of behaviors that erode trust? Might you inadvertently be doing some of these?

_____

_____

_____

_____

_____

_____

In what ways do you make tools available to your employees to achieve both professional and personal goals? In what ways could you improve?

_____

_____

Are you unintentionally protecting people from the consequences of their own behavior? If so, how can you stop?

I discussed in chapter 10, "Short, Early Conversations Make Efficient Work," how we differentiated between trust and competence, and how we found it quite useful to split these apart. I learned another benefit of trust through my efforts at making sure we did everything we could to get the *Santa Fe* sailors promoted. Of course things would go wrong from time to time, and I would have stern conversations with my team about them. These never felt bad and never felt like a me-versus-you situation because my crew knew that no matter how disappointed I seemed in their performance at the moment, I had worked tirelessly to make sure they had the best shot at getting promoted.

You can probably do more than you are.

> Are there company or industry awards for which any of my
> people might be eligible? If so, write it up and send it in.

Even if there are not specific awards, tell your boss about something great one of your people did each week. We call this "spotlight"—highlighting the accomplishments of another.

....

 Spotlight one of your employees! Send an e-mail to your boss (or write an article for the company newsletter) highlighting something one of your people did this week. Look for examples where they took initiative and responsibility; provided solutions, not just problems; and aligned their activities to the company values. Remember, when praising someone or someone's work, be specific and praise the behaviors, not personal characteristics.

....

....

RESEARCH PERSPECTIVE

When people feel supported, they can more readily focus on learning and development (Kiuru et al., 2014), as well as task performance. For a detailed breakdown of the features of trust, and a model of how trust relates to outcomes, see Colquitt et al.'s (2007) meta-analysis. They define trust as "the intention to accept vulnerability to a trustee based on positive expectations of his or her actions." This state of trusting depends on a person's general propensity to trust people, plus characteristics of the trustee. We discussed the difference between "trust" and "competence" in chapters 7, 10, and 21. Similarly, the psychology literature differentiates one's trustworthiness using the corresponding labels of "character" (for trust) and "ability" (for competence). Both dimensions make unique contributions to outcomes such as risk taking, task performance, and "citizenship behavior" (going beyond one's core job responsibilities), and they correspond with lower levels of counterproductive behaviors such as theft, sabotage, and withdrawal.

Jason A. Colquitt, Brent A. Scott, and Jeffery A. LePine, "Trust, Trustworthiness, and Trust Propensity: A Meta-Analytic Test of Their Unique Relationships with Risk Taking and Job Performance," *Journal of Applied Psychology* 92, no. 4 (2007): 909.

Noona Kiuru, et al., "Task-Focused Behavior Mediates the Associations Between Supportive Interpersonal Environments and Students' Academic Performance," *Psychological Science* 25, no. 4 (2014): 1018–24.

Chapter 22
Use Your Legacy for Clarity

Many organizations have inspiring early starts and somehow "lose their way" at some later point. I urge you to tap into the sense of purpose and urgency that developed during those early days or during some crisis. The trick is to find real ways to keep those alive as the organization grows. One of the easiest is simply to talk about them. Embed them into your guiding principles and use those words in efficiency reports and personnel awards.

 We changed the language we used for shooting torpedoes from the modern words to our World War II legacy words—running "hot, straight, and normal"—ensuring each of those meant a specific characteristic matching the modern words (pages 175–77).

MECHANISM: USE YOUR LEGACY FOR CLARITY

QUESTIONS

What is the legacy of your organization?

_____

_____

_____

_____

_____

_____

_____

How does that legacy shed light on your organization's purpose?

_____

_____

_____

_____

_____

_____

_____

What kinds of actions can you take to bring this legacy alive for individuals in your organization?

_____

_____

_____

_____

_____

As in all things, the rub lies in the execution. I had to make a conscious effort when writing awards and performance evaluations to use legacy words and avoid modern bureaucratic words.

 Gather and document stories of people doing things aligned to the company's values and culture.

Extra credit: Print a book about the history of your organization, and give it to all your employees on the anniversary of its founding. After the initial distribution, give it to all new hires.

Chapter 23
Use Guiding Principles for Decision Criteria

Guiding principles have to accurately represent the principles of the real organization, not the imagined organization. Falseness in what the organization is really about results in problems. If the guiding principles don't accurately represent the company's values, employees will make decisions that are not aligned to the organization's goals.

I have seen this, for instance, in an organization that talked about safety first but whose real interests were in profits. This organization accepted degradations in safety if they seemed "reasonable." It was a deliberate business decision, but not acknowledging that they would be balancing safety with profits resulted in miscommunication, lack of credibility (because everyone knew the truth), and misaligned decisions.

Do your guiding principles help people in your organization make day-to-day decisions? When thinking about the principles and their utility, ask yourself this question: If I was an employee faced with deciding between two different courses of action, would these principles provide me with the right criteria to select the appropriate course of action? The guiding principles need to do just that: provide guidance on decisions.

You must make sure your guiding principles are not something that just hang on a wall. You need to reinforce your principles and make them real to your employees. For example, when your company gives out awards or performance evaluations, you can express an employee's behaviors in the language of your principles.

The USS *Santa Fe* guiding principles were used to help the crew make day-to-day decisions (see pages 179–81).

MECHANISM: USE GUIDING PRINCIPLES FOR DECISION CRITERIA

QUESTIONS

Do you know your own guiding principles? Do others know them? How do you or will you communicate your principles to others?

_____

_____

_____

_____

_____

_____

_____

Use Guiding Principles for Decision Criteria

In what specific ways can you simplify your guiding principles so that everyone in your organization understands them?

_____

_____

_____

_____

_____

_____

_____

Are your guiding principles referenced in evaluations and performance awards? If they are, explain how so, and if they are not, explain how they could be incorporated and how your company might benefit from it.

_____

_____

_____

_____

_____

_____

In what ways do your guiding principles serve as decision-making criteria for your people?

_____

_____

_____

_____

_____

_____

_____

A comprehensive review of guiding principles is often looked upon as a long and painful process, but it doesn't have to be. When writing guiding principles, challenge yourself to describe the behaviors that would be manifested if people in the organization lived the principle.

Here's an example. Let's say a value of the organization is to respect each other. Imagine I had a camera and walked around the office recording conversations. What would they sound like? If someone says something that the boss thinks is odd or wrong, would the boss "correct" the person or be curious about what brought them to that conclusion? Would the person hear "tell me more" or "let me tell you why that's wrong"? The guiding principle of respect would describe people saying "tell me more" in these cases.

··

👉 For your next decision, write up how the decision aligns with your organization's guiding principles.

··

Chapter 24
Immediately Reward Desired Behaviors

Do not allow administrative processes to get in the way of prompt recognition of your employees' successes. Immediate recognition means just that, immediate. Not thirty days. Not thirty minutes. It should be immediate.

Look at your structures for awards. Are they limited? Do they pit some of your employees against others? An example of that type of award is the "employee of the month." The problem is that it isn't about being a good employee, it's about being better than the others. And only one person can win it. That structure will result in competition at the lowest level. If what you want is collaboration, then you are destroying it. Instead, have awards that are abundant, with no limit. They pit your team against the world—either external competitors or nature. I like to call these man-versus-nature as opposed to man-versus-man awards. The most important change that happens, however, is that all teams are now collaborators working for a common external goal as opposed to competitors working against one another within the same organization.

Some people worry that having a fixed objective reduces the incentive for continual improvement and breeds a mentality that "we just need to meet the goal." In some cases, this is appropriate, but in other cases, relative grading is also appropriate. There's no reason you can't do both: assign the grade based on the fixed objective and provide data on how that team stacks up against all teams. Simply providing data to the teams on their relative performance results in a natural desire to improve.

CHIEF'S PERSPECTIVE

One of the most valuable and least costly rewards you can give is immediate verbal feedback when things go well. The higher your position in the organization, the more potential impact the immediate recognition can have. If you are leading a team and they exhibit a behavior that you desire, let them know immediately and specifically what you appreciate. If your boss can deliver that immediate recognition, even better. I tried to make a point of telling my team "well done" when they exhibited the behaviors I was working toward. I would let Captain Marquet know about a specific sailor's good deeds. Then, when the captain came into sonar and recognized their work, some of the guys were stunned that the leader of the whole submarine was aware of their efforts. They thought the captain had bigger things to worry about and were truly appreciative that he took time to recognize them.

When giving praise, be specific and praise the behavior (such as attention to detail, determination, perseverance), rather than a characteristic (such as smarts or talent). The focus on behavior encourages more of that behavior. A focus on characteristics tends to make people avoid future challenges they could fail at, proving they aren't "smart" or "talented."

....

When the quick response of the throttleman saved the ship, I immediately pinned a medal on him (pages 184–85).

MECHANISM: IMMEDIATELY REWARD DESIRED BEHAVIORS

QUESTIONS

Do you have a recognition and rewards system in place that allows you to immediately applaud top performers? If you do, describe the system and the benefits you have observed from its implementation. If you do not, imagine such a system and detail how it could work within your organization.

_____

_____

_____

_____

_____

_____

How can you create scoring systems that immediately reward employees for the behaviors you want? How do you even learn that they've demonstrated those behaviors?

_____

_____

_____

_____

_____

_____

_____

There needs to be a balance between outcome and process awards. As I write this, we are in the midst of a scandal at the Veterans Administration. At several of the facilities, administrators were tinkering with waiting lists in order to make the data show an average waiting time of fewer than fourteen days. Why? Because the secretary of veterans affairs stated that fourteen days was the objective, and financial bonuses were paid to administrators in hospitals that achieved this goal.

Instead, consider process awards focused on internal actions people can take to build a system of sufficient capacity and efficiency that waiting time is reduced to fourteen days. It's what we can do every day to achieve the outcome. If there is too much emphasis on the process, then the process becomes the master and we lose sight of the outcome. If there is too much emphasis on the outcome, then we encourage shortcuts to achieve metrics.

👉 The next time someone does something that is reward worthy, issue the award immediately.

....

RESEARCH PERSPECTIVE

The closer in time a reinforcement is provided in response to desired behavior, the more quickly learning occurs. For a short history on the topic of immediacy of reinforcement (e.g., recognition), see Benjamin and Perloff's (1982) *American Psychologist* article, which discusses the role of prominent psychologists who first established the principle, such as Edward Thorndike, B. F. Skinner, and Frederick Winslow Taylor.

Ludy T. Benjamin, Jr., and Robert Perloff, "A Case of Delayed Recognition: Frederick Winslow Taylor and the Immediacy of Reinforcement," *American Psychologist* 37, no. 3 (1982): 340–2.

....

Chapter 25
Begin with the End in Mind

This mechanism's title comes from Stephen Covey's *The 7 Habits of Highly Effective People*. We had examples large and small that bore this out. When you need to be at a certain spot in the ocean at a certain time to pick up a SEAL team—your operational planning starts with that end point location and time and you then imagine the problem backward to where you are now, planning the submarine's movements so that you end up where you need to be. At the same time, we developed the practice of writing the annual performance evaluations a year ahead of time, writing what we planned to be able to write in a year.

Much of the effect of these practices was to enable us to think further out, longer term than we normally would have. This longer-term perspective was important because all investments in people are long-term investments. Without a long-term perspective, we would never see the value in taking time to develop people, and we'd just do it all ourselves—giving orders and getting through the day. Then we'd get up tomorrow and do it all over again.

The trend recently has been toward shorter and shorter contractual work relationships. A shorter-term relationship between employee and employer reduces the motivation for companies to invest in employee training. I might guess that the burden for training will fall upon the individual more.

It took ten years to realize the full impact of what we had done by creating all the leaders we had.

I find many business leaders who tell me that change is happening faster and faster, and that it's more important to develop an organization that is adaptable than one that plans far out into the future. That's true for things like products, processes, and technology—but investing in people still moves no faster than our biological clocks.

One of the ways we implemented "begin with the end in mind" was the practice of writing the annual performance evaluations and end-of-tour awards for one and three years hence (pages 190–91).

MECHANISM: BEGIN WITH THE END IN MIND

QUESTIONS

For how far in the future are you optimizing your organization? What about the people above and below you in the organization?

_____

_____

_____

_____

_____

_____
_____

In what ways are you mentoring solely to instruct? In what ways do you mentor to learn as well?

_____
_____
_____
_____
_____
_____

How will you know if you have accomplished your organizational and personal goals? Are you measuring the things you need to be?

_____
_____
_____
_____
_____
_____

Have you assigned a team to write up the company's goals three to five years out? If you have, how did your team handle this task, and in what ways were the results lacking or satisfactory? To what degree did the plan talk about products and market share, and to what degree did the

plan talk about people taking on increased responsibility and development?

_____
_____
_____
_____
_____
_____

In what ways can you reward staff members who attain their measurable goals?

_____
_____
_____
_____
_____
_____

What steps can you take in order to redesign your management team's
schedule so you can mentor one another?

_____
_____
_____
_____
_____
_____

Begin with the End in Mind

ACTIVITY: LONG-TERM THINKING

Long-term thinking is a practice. Here are some things you can do to begin with the end in mind.

1.   Hand out chapter 25, "Looking Ahead," in *Turn the Ship Around!* (pages 188–94) as reading material. Also consider having your people read Stephen Covey's book *The 7 Habits of Highly Effective People,* chapter 2, "Begin with the End in Mind" (pages 96–144).

2.   Discuss the concepts and idea of "begin with the end in mind." With your leadership team, develop long-term organizational goals for three to five years out.

3.   Go through the goals and look for statements that express achievement. In every case, ask, "How would we know?" and ensure that you have measuring systems in place.

4.   Then have employees write their own goals one year, two years, or three years hence. The goals in the employees' evaluations should cascade down from the organization's goals; they needn't necessarily be identical but should be appropriate at an individual level.

5.   Have conversations with employees to make their achievements indisputable ("How would I know?") and measurable.

As you work with individuals in your organization to develop their vision for the future, it is helpful to establish specific, measurable goals. These goals will help the individuals realize their ambitions.

....

☞ Write your next performance evaluation now.

....

Chapter 26

Encourage a Questioning Attitude
over Blind Obedience

*What is done without question is done blindly. Discourage
blind obedience by encouraging a questioning attitude.*

Are you looking for resilience in your organization? We realized aboard
the *Santa Fe* that resilience and effectiveness sometimes meant questioning orders. There are circumstances where the person in charge is about
to mistakenly issue an order, because he either does not have all the relevant
facts to make the right decision or has drawn an incorrect conclusion based
on an incorrect assumption. It is the duty of your people to speak up to
correct the situation before the mistake is made that would cause significant
negative consequences.

We found that this behavior was more likely after we'd implemented
Intent-Based Leadership than before. Somehow, all the practice crew members

had, in thinking and making their own decisions, made it easier to question the (few) times I gave orders.

At the 2017 Academy Awards, Warren Beatty and Faye Dunaway were the presenters for best picture, the last award of the evening. A critical error occurred when the PricewaterhouseCoopers accountant who held the envelopes of the winners incorrectly gave the envelope for best actress to Warren Beatty. The envelope Beatty had was labeled on the outside "Actress in a Leading Role," the award that was just presented to Emma Stone. Beatty and Dunaway started the preamble and announced the nominees and stood on stage for the trailers. Four minutes passed, but Beatty didn't look at the envelope to check. He had no reason to suspect anything was amiss. Inside, the card said "Emma Stone, *La La Land*."

When Beatty opened the envelope and looked at the card he recognized that something was wrong. Why would the card for best picture have the name Emma Stone on it? In very small font at the bottom of the card were the words "Actress in a Leading Role"—but noticing this would have required Beatty to scrutinize the card. Beatty looked in the envelope again, he paused, and then he started into the script for the award. When he showed the card to Faye Dunaway, she immediately said "*La La Land*." Beatty knew something was wrong but said later he thought it was a typo. He didn't stop the ceremony. Dunaway didn't question the card and read the name of the movie.

While the prime failure was that of the PwC accountant, Dunaway and Beatty could have prevented the error with a more questioning attitude and a preplanned process to pause the proceedings in the event of a question. Since there is great ritual and fanfare about the preparation of the winner's envelopes, everyone's mental framework was that it "had" to be right. It's human nature not to think things could go wrong.

ACTIVITY 1: WHAT THE ACADEMY AWARDS TEACH ABOUT HIGH-RELIABILITY ORGANIZATIONS

Find a clip of the failed Academy Awards presentation and watch it with your team. Ask the following questions: How would you write the job description for Faye Dunaway and Warren Beatty as you believe they understood it to be? Question two: Why didn't Warren Beatty stop the ceremony when he was confused by the incorrect card? The answers are keys to developing a high-reliability organization.

 The SEAL team rendezvous demonstrated the power of questioning orders (pages 197–200).

MECHANISM: ENCOURAGE A QUESTIONING ATTITUDE OVER BLIND OBEDIENCE

QUESTIONS

Do you want obedience or effectiveness? In what ways is your organization currently structured to encourage one more than the other?

_____

_____

_____

_____

_____

_____

Will your people follow an incorrect order simply because it is an order? How would you build a culture in your workplace that embraces a questioning attitude where such an order would be challenged?

_____

_____

_____

_____

_____

_____

_____

ACTIVITY 2: DISSENT WITHOUT DISTRUST

Based on research conducted by Solomon Asch in the 1950s on what is called the Conformity Theory,* we learned that even when people know something is the wrong answer, they will agree with the group essentially a third of the time. This is called conformity bias. However, if even one person disagrees with the group, whether their answer is right or wrong, it makes it safe for others to dissent, thus breaking the spell of the conformity bias. We want to break away from the conformity bias by practicing dissent in our workplaces.

In the military, we have an activity called "red-teaming" a decision during which we formally set up a team to take an alternative perspective on a challenging issue. You might not need to go this far to formalize the procedure, but you do want to get your team practicing being comfortable with dissent.

You can perform the following activity with your team:

....

*S. E. Asch, "Studies of Independence and Conformity: I. A Minority of One Against a Unanimous Majority," _Psychological Monographs_ 70 (1956): 1–70.

Encourage a Questioning Attitude over Blind Obedience

1. During your next meeting, when you begin to talk about a position, or start to make a significant decision, pass out red and black cards facedown to your employees. This activity generally works best with an 8:2 ratio of black to red. Individuals who receive a black card have the option to agree or dissent, but anyone who receives a red card must dissent. It is important when you start this activity to inform the participants that they will reveal their cards at the end to ease participants' concerns about their dissent being perceived as "difficult" or reflecting poorly on them.

2. People who receive a red card will be the dissenters, and their job will be to ask questions, challenge assumptions, or overtly state something that seems contrary to the direction that the group is moving in, even if they do not personally believe it. Even if a red-card holder agrees with the group's decision, the objective of the activity is simply to flex the "opposing-view muscle" through practice.

3. If you practice this for a couple of weeks, you can then go to the next phase: don't reveal the cards at the end of the meeting.

PRACTICAL RESULTS

What we think you'll find is that you won't need to use the cards for very long, and eventually the cards can go away. As you continue to go through this activity, you will find that three things happen:

First, as people practice dissenting and practice understanding what words to use in collective situations to challenge the rest of the group, they will become more comfortable with both the idea and the execution of dissent. They will figure out language that alerts the group to a dissenting idea without shutting everyone else's ears to what they have to say.

Examples of some language of dissent:

- "I'm going to challenge the group here . . ."
- "I see things a bit differently . . ."
- "I want to bring up a different opinion . . ."

Second, everyone in the group hears their coworkers when they dissent and sees that the environment is safe for them too to challenge a decision. That's the behavior you want and what you're hopefully going to end up with through practice.

Finally, it breaks the false link between dissent and distrust, allowing disagreement over what we see, interpret, and recommend while maintaining common goals.

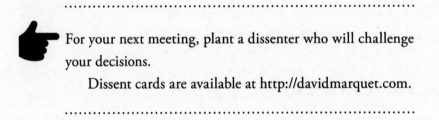

For your next meeting, plant a dissenter who will challenge your decisions.

Dissent cards are available at http://davidmarquet.com.

Chapter 27
Implementing Intent-Based Leadership and Building Leaders at Every Level

The core of Intent-Based Leadership is giving employees control over what they work on and how they work. It means letting them make meaningful decisions. The two enabling pillars are competence and clarity.

I worry that some readers will think of the list of mechanisms as prescriptions that, if followed, will result in the same long-term systematic improvements we saw on the *Santa Fe*. I don't think so. In my work as a business consultant, I have come to appreciate how much each organization is different and unique. The people making up the organization have different backgrounds and a different level of tolerance for responsibility and a different sense of comfort in emancipation.

Your mechanisms will be structurally similar, but the specifics will be different. We found that one of the most important mechanisms for control was to change the level in the organization where an individual's vacation was approved. In your organization, it may not be the vacation policy. It may be the level at which discounts are approved for the customer. It may be the dollar amount an employee can obligate without higher authority. It may be whom a call center employee calls next and how far they can deviate from the script. If you ask your people what authorities they would like in order to make their jobs easier, you'll definitely get some ideas.

MECHANISM: IMPLEMENT INTENT-BASED LEADERSHIP

QUESTIONS

Are you ready to take the first steps toward Intent-Based Leadership and an empowered and engaged workforce? What will these first steps look like for your company and your people?

_____

_____

_____

_____

_____

_____

Which mechanisms from the *Santa Fe* are most immediately applicable to your organization?

_____

_____

_____

_____

_____

_____

_____

Implementing Intent-Based Leadership

In what ways do you have the stamina for long-term thinking? When situations occur that trigger your own past leader-follower behaviors, what will you do to stay focused on the long term?

_____

_____

_____

_____

_____

_____

_____

PART V
Final Mechanism and Conclusions

Chapter 28
Don't Empower, Emancipate

Empowerment is only a necessary step because we've been accustomed to disempowerment. Empowerment is needed to undo all those top-down, do-what-you're-told, be-a-team-player messages that result from our leader-follower model. But empowerment isn't enough.

First, empowerment by itself is not a complete leadership structure. Empowerment does not work without the attributes of competence and clarity. Second, empowerment still results from and is a manifestation of a top-down structure. At its core is the belief that the leader "empowers" the followers, that the leader has the power and ability to empower the followers. We need more than that because empowerment within a leader-follower structure is a modest compensation for the overwhelming signal that "you are a follower." It is a confusing signal.

What we need is release, or emancipation. Emancipation is fundamentally different from empowerment. With emancipation we recognize the inherent genius, energy, and creativity in all people and allow those talents to emerge. We realize that we don't have the power to give these talents to others, or to "empower" them to use them, only the power to prevent them from coming out. Emancipation results when teams have been given decision-making control and have the additional characteristics of competence and clarity. You know you have an emancipated team when you no longer feel the need to empower them. Indeed, you no longer have the ability to empower them because they are not relying on you as their source of power.

....

CHIEF'S PERSPECTIVE

One of the greatest results of emancipating your teams is that psychological ownership shifts to your team. When Captain Marquet moved authority to levels where the information was, some feared that people would fail to consider how decisions would impact others. Exactly the opposite happened. Team leaders with new authority started to make decisions based on how it would affect everyone on the team.

....

MECHANISM: DON'T EMPOWER, EMANCIPATE

QUESTIONS
In what ways are you limiting your leadership to empowerment?

_____

_____

_____

_____

_____

_____

_____

What programs have you instituted or could you institute in order to supplement control with competence and clarity?

_____

_____

_____

_____

_____

_____

In what ways have you divested yourself of the attitude that you, as a corporate leader, will empower your staff? What steps could you take to further divest yourself?

_____

_____

_____

_____

_____

_____

_____

When I arrived as the captain of the *Santa Fe,* I spent twenty hours a day running around making hundreds of decisions and doing a lot. There was no time to think and no time to develop people. I needed to look at what I was doing and devise ways to delegate it to others. I wanted to pare back my activities to those things that only I could do. I eventually ended up with this list. I was the only one who could:

Maintain my personal relationships.

Maintain my own level of technical competence.

Influence the environment that sets the culture.

Interact in a positive way with my immediate reports.

Everything else, I could delegate.

....

CHIEF'S PERSPECTIVE

Captain Marquet's list is very similar to the list that applies to people in the middle of the organization. Controlling others, no matter your position in an organization, is virtually impossible. The one thing you can control is yourself. Building your competence, maintaining your relationships with others, fostering a positive environment, and developing others is completely in your control. As you display your competence, clarity, and desire to foster a great environment, your leader will find it safe to start giving you control over your work. It happened quickly on the *Santa Fe,* but it can take time, especially in teams that are used to top-down control.

....

As a team member, in what ways are you displaying your competence and clarity?

_____

_____

Don't Empower, Emancipate

_____

_____

_____

_____

_____

....

👉 What is on your plate this week? Take one thing and delegate it.

....

Chapter 29
Ripples

I hope that you have the success that we saw on board the USS *Santa Fe*. Some of what you will see will be obvious and quick. But some of the impacts will take time and patience to see. Yet these will be the most important things that you do for the people you touch in your life—creating environments where they can be great just the way they are, and having them believe that.

Intent-Based Leadership Manifesto

We live by these principles . . .

We view people as our purpose, not as a means.

We commit to leading in a way that invites people to think, not in a way that gets people to do.

We commit to creating environments where people can be great, just the way they are, instead of trying to "fix" people.

We recognize that we don't see everything and commit to being curious about what others see and think.

We commit to leadership that creates additional leaders and reject the idea that leaders attract followers.

We commit to pushing authority to information, instead of pushing information to authority.

We understand that we will fail to live up to our commitments and appreciate our own fallibility, resolving to try again.

We will frequently evaluate what we do and how we do it. Anything not awesome will be improved. We will strive to get better, never protecting a reputation for being good.

Appendix: Summary of Practices from *Turn the Ship Around!*

STARTING OVER

Identify your assumptions and question your preconceptions of leadership.

Think long term.

CONTROL

Find the genetic code for control and rewrite it.

Act your way to new thinking.

Short, early conversations make efficient work.

Use "I intend to . . ." to turn passive followers into active leaders.

Resist the urge to provide solutions.

Appendix: Summary of Practices

Eliminate top-down monitoring systems.

Think out loud (both superiors and subordinates).

Embrace the inspectors.

COMPETENCE

Take deliberate action.

We learn (everywhere, all the time).

Don't brief, certify.

Continually and consistently repeat the message.

Specify goals, not methods.

CLARITY

Achieve excellence, don't just avoid errors.

Build trust and take care of your people.

Use your legacy for clarity.

Use guiding principles for decision criteria.

Use immediate rewards to reinforce desired behaviors.

Begin with the end in mind.

Encourage a questioning attitude over blind obedience.

Acknowledgments

I am deeply indebted to leaders everywhere who have ever tried to make the world a better place for others.

I have been fueled by readers of *Turn the Ship Around!* who have shared their own stories with me.

I would like to specifically thank the following for their assistance on the workbook: Ashleigh Riddle, Kim Harrison, Jon Kirk, Jenni Jepsen, Christopher Wells, Dan Osborne, and the highly capable team at Portfolio / Penguin.

I would like to thank our initial production and design partner Heather Granader for her cheery, creative, and proactive work.

For this edition, I acknowledge the dedicated research of Dr. Mike Gillespie, who provided the Research Perspectives, and the writing of Andy Worshek, who shared his Chief's Perspectives.

In particular, I thank my mentor and friend Simon Sinek for his help imagining a world that might be.

For additional help with Intent-Based Leadership:

Enroll to get your leadership nudges™, sixty-second reminders
of Intent-Based Leadership principles and practices, at
www.davidmarquet.com.

Subscribe to the Leadership Nudge YouTube channel and Facebook
page or follow @leadershipnudge.

You can connect with me @ldavidmarquet on Twitter and on Facebook.

For information on bringing an Intent-Based Leadership seminar to
your workplace, email chuck@turntheshiparound.com

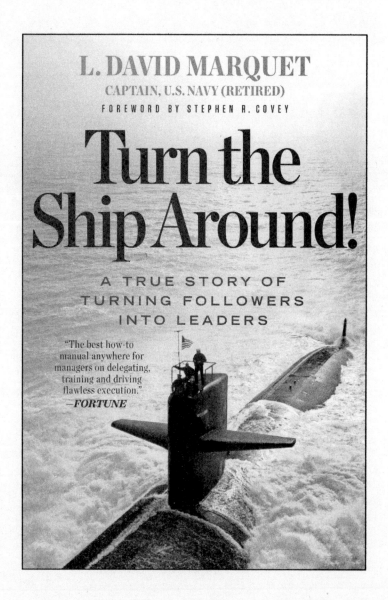